Prime Ski Racing

Prime Ski Racing

Triumph of the Racer's Mind

Jim Taylor, Ph.D.

Writers Club Press
San Jose New York Lincoln Shanghai

Also by Dr. Jim Taylor

Prime Sport
Prime Tennis
Prime Golf
The Mental Edge for Skiing
Psychology of Dance
Psychological Approaches to Sports Injury Rehabilitation
Comprehensive Sports Injury Management

Prime Ski Racing
Triumph of the Racer's Mind

Writers Club Press
an imprint of iUniverse.com, Inc.

For information address:
iUniverse.com, Inc.
5220 S 16th, Ste. 200
Lincoln, NE 68512
www.iuniverse.com

Cover design by Gerald Sindell and Jim Taylor, Ph.D.

ISBN: 0-595-13993-0

Printed in the United States of America

To order books by Dr. Jim Taylor or
for information about consultation and workshops contact:

Jim Taylor, Ph.D.
Alpine/Taylor Consulting
P.O. Box 475313 San Francisco, CA 94147
tel: 415.345.9820 fax: 415.345.9830
e-mail: jtphd@alpinetaylor.com
web site: www.alpinetaylor.com

ACKNOWLEDGEMENTS

Special thanks to Gerald Sindell, my manager, mentor, and friend. His creative and critical input to this book has been essential, and his support, vision, and perspective in my career and life have been invaluable.

I would like to thank the thousands of racers and coaches with whom I have worked over the past 15 years. They have been my teachers.

Finally, I would like to express my love and appreciation to my parents, Ceci and Shel Taylor, for instilling in me a passion for maximizing human performance, which has become the focal point of my life's work.

CONTENTS

PREFACE

When you race, you will, in fact, be competing in two races. The obvious race is the competitive one that occurs against the rest of the field. The more important race, though, is the mental race that you have inside your head against yourself. Here is a simple reality: If you don't win the mental race, you won't ski well in the competitive race.

Contrary to what many racers may think, at whatever level in which they're competing, the technical and physical aspects of ski racing don't usually determine the winner. Racers who compete at the same level are very similar technically and physically. For example, is Herman Maier better technically than Michael Von Gruenigen? Is Pernilla Wilberg in better physical condition than Kristina Koznick? In both cases, the answer is clearly no. This is probably true for you and your biggest competitors as well. So, on any given day, what separates a Stefan Eberharter from a Kristian Ghedina, or you from your greatest competitors? The answer lies in who wins the mental race. Racers who are the most motivated to ski their best, who have the greatest confidence in themselves, who ski best under pressure, who stay focused on their racing, and who keep their emotions under control will most often emerge victorious.

Whenever I talk to serious racers, I ask them what aspect of their ski racing seems to have the greatest impact on how they ski. Almost unanimously they say the mental part of ski racing. I then ask how much time they put into their mental preparation. Their answer is almost always, little or no time.

Despite its obvious importance, the mental side of ski racing is most often neglected, at least until a problem arises. The mistake racers make is that they don't treat the mental race the way they treat the physical and technical aspects of ski racing. They don't wait to get injured before they do physical conditioning. They don't develop a technical flaw before they work on their technique. Rather, they do physical and technical training to prevent problems from arising. Racers should approach the mental race in the same way.

Prime Ski Racing was created to assist you in just this process, ensuring that mentally you are your best ally rather than your worst enemy. *Prime Ski Racing* focuses on the essentials of the mental race and shows you how to make your mind work for you instead of against you.

Prime Ski Racing is not magic dust and will not produce miracles. You would not expect increases in strength by lifting weights a few times or an improvement in technique by working on it for a few hours. The only way to improve any area, whether physical, technical, or mental, is through commitment, hard work, and patience.

Prime Ski Racing describes issues and problems that are common to racers regardless of their ability or experience, and are most likely also important to you. The information, techniques, and exercises in *Prime Ski Racing* are designed to be "user-friendly;" easy to understand and apply directly to racing. My goal is for you to read *Prime Ski Racing* and go out tomorrow and use it immediately to improve your skiing.

The information and strategies described in *Prime Ski Racing* are not really ski racing skills or even sport psychology skills. Rather, they are life skills that can be used to enhance any part of your life. *Prime Ski Racing* can be used in your racing or any area you choose to improve your performance and achieve your goals.

Prime Ski Racing has several goals. First, to provide clear and understandable information about winning the mental race. Second, to offer simple and practical techniques that you can easily use to raise your skiing to a new level. Finally, to enable you to ski your best consistently.

> *"It's a mental thing. There's a psychological zone I have to discover to ski my best."*
>
> **World championship medallist AJ Kitt**

USING PRIME SKI RACING

There's a great deal of information in *Prime Ski Racing*. You shouldn't expect to take in and use all of the information the first time you read this book. Winning the mental race is a process that will parallel your own ski racing development. It takes time to develop your physical and technical abilities. It will also take time to win the mental race.

Prime Ski Racing has been specifically designed to make it easy for you to understand and use its information and techniques. It is organized around what I believe to be the most important mental issues that impact ski racing. This structure enables you to select the areas most relevant to your ski racing. It allows you to find out exactly what you need to know for where you are in your ski racing participation and development. *Prime Ski Racing* describes in detail the skills you need to develop for the mental areas that are most important to you. It shows you the exercises you need to practice to win the mental race.

I would suggest the following process in using *Prime Ski Racing* to its greatest benefit. First, read the book all of the way through. As you read, make note of specific topics that are currently important to you. After reading the entire book, identify the issues that are most important to you and re-read those sections to better familiarize yourself with them. Then, select two or three areas on which you want to work. Experiment with different techniques to develop the areas you've chosen and select the ones you like best. Finally, implement those techniques in your daily schedule.

Now let's begin the exciting journey that culminates in the "triumph of the racer's mind."

> *"A winner is not one who has the best balance, coordination, and skill, and uses these talents in competitive sports; that person is an athlete. A winner is one who among all the others with equal skills, is able to go beyond his inhibitions to reach out and touch perfection, and bring that experience to his life, and manifest it in his sport."*
>
> **Former U.S. Ski Team member Scott Dorwart**

SECTION I

INTRODUCTION

To begin *Prime Ski Racing*, I would like to introduce you to several key concepts that will act as the foundation for the remainder of this book. One of the most popular phrases used in sport psychology is *peak performance*, which is typically defined as the highest level of performance an athlete can achieve, and it's considered to be the goal toward which all athletes should strive. When I came out of graduate school, peak performance was what I wanted the racers with whom I worked to achieve.

But as I became more experienced as a psychologist and as a writer, I began to appreciate the power of words and how important it is that the words I use are highly descriptive of what I want to communicate. I decided that peak performance was not descriptive of what I wanted to convey to the racers with whom I worked. I saw several problems with peak performance. One difficulty is that racers can only maintain a peak for a very short time. Would you be satisfied if you skied well in one race and then did poorly in subsequent ones? Also, once that peak is reached, there is only one way to go, and that is down. And with most peaks, the drop is steep and fast.

So I needed to find a phrase that accurately described what I wanted racers to achieve. I struggled for several years unable to find such a phrase until one day a meeting of luck and readiness occurred. Walking through the meat section of a grocery store I saw a piece of beef with a sticker that read Prime Cut. I had an "aha" experience. I knew I was on to something.

I returned to my office and looked up "prime" in the dictionary. It was defined as "of the highest quality or value." I had finally found the phrase, "Prime Performance," which I believed was highly descriptive of what I wanted racers to achieve.

I defined Prime Performance, or in this case, Prime Ski Racing, as "performing at a consistently high level under the most challenging conditions." There are two essential words in this definition. The first key word is, "consistently." I'm not interested if a racer can have only one or two great races. That is not enough to be truly successful. I want racers to be able to ski at a high level day in and day out, week in and week out, month in and month out. This doesn't mean performing perfectly. Rather, it means performing at a high level with only minimal ups and downs instead of the large swings in performance that are so common among racers. The second key word is, "challenging." I'm not impressed if a racer can ski well under ideal conditions against easy competition when they are well-rested and skiing their best. Anyone can do that. What makes the great racers successful is their ability to ski their best under the worst possible conditions against tough competition when they're not skiing their best. If the racers with whom I worked could attain this level of performance, Prime Ski Racing, they would be successful.

A question you may ask is, Where does Prime Ski Racing come from? Though I'll be focusing on its mental contributors, the mind is only one necessary part of Prime Ski Racing. You must also be at a high level of physical health including being well-conditioned, well-rested, eating a balanced diet, and free from injury and illness. Prime Ski Racing is also not possible if you're not technically sound. Your technical skills must be well-learned and your tactics must be ingrained. If you're physically, technically, tactically, and mentally prepared, then you will have the ability to achieve Prime Ski Racing.

Now here is a question for you: Have you ever experienced Prime Ski Racing? Do you know what it feels like to ski at that level? Let me describe some of the common experiences of Prime Ski Racing. First, Prime Ski

Racing is effortless. It's comfortable, easy, and natural. You don't seem to have to try to do anything. Prime Ski Racing is also automatic. There's little thought. The body does what it knows how to do and there's no mental interference getting in the way. You also experience sharpened senses. You see, hear, and feel everything more acutely than normal. Also, time seems to slow down, enabling you to react more quickly. I've heard World Cup racers say that when they're skiing well, everything seems to be moving in slow motion. At those times, they are experiencing Prime Ski Racing. Prime Ski Racing also has effortless focus. You're totally absorbed in the experience and are focused entirely on the process. You have no distractions or unnecessary thoughts that interfere with your skiing your best. You have boundless energy. Your endurance seems endless and fatigue is simply not an issue. Finally, you experience what I call prime integration. Everything is working together. The physical, technical, tactical, and mental aspects of ski racing are integrated into one path to Prime Ski Racing.

> *"It's way mental. The biggest thing is the psychological aspect of believing I can go out and give it 100 percent. When I'm going for it really aggressively I ski my best. The toughest part is finding that zone."*

Olympic champion Tommy Moe

PHILOSOPHY OF PRIME SKI RACING

Before you can begin the process of developing Prime Ski Racing, you need to create a foundation of beliefs about your ski racing on which you can build your mental skills. This foundation involves your attitudes in three areas. First, your perspective on competition; what you think of it, how you feel about it, and how you approach it. Second, your view of yourself as a competitor; do you ski better in training, races, or big events? Third, your attitude toward winning and losing; how you define winning and losing, and whether you know the essential roles that both winning and losing play in becoming the best ski racer you can be. Clarifying your views in these three areas will make it easier to win the mental race and to achieve Prime Ski Racing.

PRIME SKI RACING PERSPECTIVE ON COMPETITION

Ski racing is obviously important to you. You put a great deal of effort in your ski racing. Because of this, you put your ego on the line every time you get in the starting gate. When you don't ski well, you're disappointed. This may not feel good, but it's natural because it means you care about your ski racing.

There is, however, a point at which racers can lose perspective and their feelings toward their racing can hurt their performances. The key warning signal of this overinvolvement is "too." When they care *too* much, when it is *too* important to them, when they try *too* hard to win, when they press *too* much in critical races, then they have lost perspective.

In this "too" situation, racers' investment in their skiing is so great that it is no longer enjoyable. If you find yourself feeling this way, you should reevaluate what your ski racing means to you and how it impacts your life and your happiness. You will probably find that it plays too big a role in how you feel about yourself. When this happens, you not only ski poorly and have worse results, but you may find that ski racing is no longer fun to you.

To ski your best and to have fun, you need to keep your ski racing participation in perspective. It may be important to you, but it should not be life or death. What is important is that you have a balanced view of ski racing. Remember why you participate; it's fun, it feels great to become a good skier, and, yes, you like to compete and win. The Prime Ski Racing view of competition means keeping your ski racing in perspective. If you have fun, work hard, enjoy the process of ski racing, and do not care too much about winning and losing, you will enjoy ski racing more, you will ski better, and you will have better results as well

> *"I have never made sports bigger than life. I just played and enjoyed them. My whole approach was based on what I could learn from sports."*
> **NFL quarterback Rick Mirer**

UPS AND DOWNS OF SKI RACING

Another aspect of the Prime Ski Racing perspective on racing is recognizing and accepting its ups and downs. In the history of ski racing, very few racers have had perfect or near-perfect seasons: Franz Klammer, Ingemar Stenmark. Even the best racers have ups and downs. Since they do, then you should expect to have them too. It's not whether you have ups and downs in your ski racing, but how big the ups and downs are and how you respond to them. In fact, *Prime Ski Racing* is devoted to assisting you in minimizing the ups and downs of ski racing.

In a down period, it's easy to get frustrated, angry, and depressed. You can feel really disappointed in how you're skiing and can feel helpless to change it. You may want to just give up. But none of these feelings will help you accomplish your important goals: getting out of the down period and returning to a high level of performance. This is a skill that separates the great racers from the good ones. The best racers know how to get back to an up period quickly.

How do they do this? First, they keep the down period in perspective, knowing that it's a natural and expected part of ski racing. This attitude takes the pressure off them to rush back to a higher level of performance and keeps them from getting too upset. It also enables them to stay positive and motivated. Most importantly, they never give up. They keep working hard, no matter how bad it gets. These racers look for the cause of their slump and then find a solution. If you maintain this attitude toward the ups and downs of ski racing, your down periods won't last as long and you'll more quickly swing back to an up period.

> *"When I've had problems this year, I've been able to dig down and charge. You have to make the best of any situation."*

> **Former USST member Jennifer Collins**

SKI RACING IS ABOUT LOVE AND FUN

It's easy to lose sight of why you compete in ski racing. There are the trophies, rankings, and attention. Yet, when you get focused on the external benefits of ski racing, you may lose sight of the internal reasons why you compete. You may not have as much fun and you won't ski as well either. When this happens, you need to remind yourself of what ski racing is all about. Ski racing is about two things. First, it is about love: love of ski racing, love of others, and love of yourself. If you love ski racing, you have a chance to achieve Prime Ski Racing.

Second, ski racing is about fun. Working hard, improving your skiing, the joy of racing, and enjoying the process, win or lose, should all be fun. If you always remember that ski racing is about love and fun, then you will enjoy participating and you will ski your best.

> *"I love ski racing and that's important. If you don't, either you have to figure out a way to do it or you might as well hang it up. You're not going to be a contender if you're not enjoying yourself."*

> **USST member Casey Puckett**

PRIME SKI RACING FOR WINNING AND LOSING

Related to your attitude toward competition is your approach to winning and losing. How you define winning and losing, and your perceptions of the roles that winning and losing play in developing Prime Ski Racing, will determine your ability to ski your best consistently.

Too often, winning and losing are defined narrowly with only one winner and many losers. The racer who wins the race is the winner and everyone else is a loser. But how many times have you skied well, yet lost. The fact is you can't usually control whether you win or lose. What you can control is the effort you put in and how well you ski. It's fruitless to strive for something that's out of your control, so winning and losing should be defined in terms of things over which you have control. With this in mind, I define winning as giving your best effort and performing to the best of your ability. I define losing as not trying your hardest and not performing as well as you can. The nice thing about this definition is that it's within your control, you'll feel less pressure, you'll ski better, and as a result, you will probably win more.

> *"Michael Jordan told me once that you have to learn how to fail before you can learn to succeed."*
>
> **Shaquille O'Neal**

MYTH AND REALITY OF WINNING AND LOSING

There are many myths and misconceptions that racers hold about winning and losing. Many racers believe that the only way to win is to have always won; that winners rarely lose and losers always lose. The reality is that winners lose more often than losers. Losers lose a few times and quit. Winners lose at first, learn from the losses, then begin to win because of what they've learned.

Both winning and losing are essential to becoming a consistent winner. Winning builds confidence and reinforces racers' belief that they can ski well and at a high level. There are, however, problems with winning too much and too early. Winning can breed complacency because, if racers win all of the time, there's little motivation to improve. Sooner or later though, as they move up the competitive ladder, they'll come up against someone who is just as good or better than them, and since they haven't improved their skiing, they won't be successful against them. Winning also doesn't identify areas in need of improvement. If racers always win, their weaknesses won't become apparent and they won't see the need to work on their skiing . Winning also doesn't teach racers how to constructively handle the inevitable obstacles and setbacks of ski racing. Racers will be so accustomed to winning that when they finally do lose, it will be a shock to them.

There are also benefits to losing that will ultimately enable racers to win more. Losing provides racers with information about their progress. It shows racers what they're doing well and, more importantly, what they need to improve on. Losing also shows racers what doesn't work, which helps them identify what works best. Losing also teaches racers how to positively handle adversity.

Rather than becoming discouraged by losing, you should focus on how it will help you become a better ski racer. If you learn the valuable lessons from both winning and losing, you'll gain the perspective toward ski racing that will allow you to achieve Prime Ski Racing.

PRIME SKI RACING COMPETITOR

Being the best ski racer you can takes more than being in great physical condition and being technically skilled. There are many racers who have those qualities, but don't ski to the best of their ability. There are many junior champions who never became stars on the World Cup. Performing your best requires that you have all of the normal things you would expect a great ski racer to have: physically well-conditioned, excellent technique, sound tactics, and the latest equipment. That is not enough though; those things will only make you a good ski racer. You need more to become your best. You need to become a Prime Ski Racing competitor.

There's a big difference between being able to ski well in training, in races, and in important events such as the Junior Olympics or the national championships. This difference is what separates racers from Prime Ski Racing competitors. It's difficult enough getting into good physical condition, developing good technical skills, and understanding the tactical aspects of ski racing. The final challenge is learning how to evolve from a racer to a Prime Ski Racing competitor.

LEVELS OF COMPETITIVE SKI RACING

There are three levels at which you can compete. The first level is as a *racer*. Racers are technically solid and generally ski well in training, but they don't usually ski up to their ability in races. They ski even worse under pressure. Racers typically only have good results when they're better than most of their competition and they never win races.

The next level of skiing is as a *performer*. Performers ski adequately in training and ski well in most races. They can be counted on to have good results. Performers, however, are rarely able to get that big win that propels them to top. They don't respond well to the pressures of competition. They're unable to harness the pressure and raise their skiing when the race is on the line. Simply put, performers don't ski their best when it really counts.

The ultimate level is as a Prime Ski Racing *competitor*. Prime Ski Racing competitors don't always ski well in training. They may even occasionally lose in less important races. But what separates Prime Ski Racing competitors from racers and performers is how they respond to pressure. In big races against tough competition, their skiing rises to a new level. Everything that turns negative for racers and performers shifts positively for Prime Ski Racing competitors. They thrive on the pressure of important races and ski their best against the most difficult competition and in the worst conditions. Prime Ski Racing competitors win the big races on the tough hills that propel them to the top.

QUALITIES OF A PRIME SKI RACING COMPETITOR

Looking back at the great ski racers over the years from Jean-Claude Killy and Nancy Greene to Gustavo Thoeni and Annemarie Proell to Herman Maier and Deborah Campagnoni, you see in them common qualities that made them Prime Ski Racing competitors. Each had unique abilities, styles, and personalities, but all shared several essential characteristics.

At the heart of all Prime Ski Racing competitors is an unwavering determination to be the best. They are driven to get better and better. They have a great passion for hard work. They spend hours training every day to improve their skiing. They love the grind and repetition of training and they are willing to suffer to succeed. Most basically, their love of ski racing precedes their love of competing and winning.

Prime Ski Racing competitors have a deep and enduring belief in themselves. They have the confidence to take risks, to do seemingly impossible things, and to never give up no matter what. This belief enables them to be inspired rather than discouraged by defeat and allows them to keep faith in their ability even when they are not skiing their best. Difficult conditions and tough competition are exciting challenges and opportunities to showcase their skills.

Prime Ski Racing competitors are able to raise their performances when they need to in order to win. They seem to thrive on pressure of the "big race" like the World Championships. They have the ability to stay calm and focused with an Olympic gold medal on the line. Most fundamentally, Prime Ski Racing competitors ski their best in the most important races of their lives.

> *"The most important thing is to be convinced of your chances."*
>
> **Olympic champion Alberto Tomba**

HOW TO BECOME A PRIME SKI RACING COMPETITOR

Becoming a Prime Ski Racing competitor requires that you maximize every aspect of your ski racing ability. It starts at the physical level. You must be in the best possible physical condition of which you're capable. Next, you have to develop your technical skills. You need to have your technique so well ingrained and automatic, that it holds up when the pressure is on. You must also be tactically skilled, knowing the best strategy for the race conditions in which you find yourself. So far, though, this will only enable you to become a performer at best. It is the next step that will put you on the path to becoming a Prime Ski Racing competitor.

You need to be highly motivated to put in the time and effort necessary to be physically, technically, and tactically prepared. You must develop the confidence that you can ski your best in the most important race of your life under the most demanding conditions in which you have ever competed. You need to train yourself to seek out and thrive on pressure and have the ability to stay calm and focused when the race is on the line. Lastly, you must have the ability to use your emotions to your advantage so that they help you ski your best.

Prime Ski Racing is devoted to helping you achieve this part of becoming a Prime Ski Racing competitor. You must be totally prepared for every race: physically, technically, tactically, and mentally ready to ski your best. If you can develop yourself in these areas, you will become a Prime Ski Racing competitor.

> *"At the upper levels, mental preparation is the difference between winners and losers."*
>
> **Former USST member Zach Crist**

PRIME SKI RACING SKILLS ARE SKILLS

Many racers have misconceptions about the mental side of ski racing. Racers often believe that mental abilities are inborn, in other words, racers either have them or they don't, and if not, they can't develop them. But mental abilities are skills, just like technical skills, that can be developed. You should approach Prime Ski Racing skills the same way you approach physical and technical parts of your ski racing. If you work on them, your Prime Ski Racing skills will improve and your overall race performances will be raised.

> *"My physical skills may not be as good as they were in 1988, but my mental skills are so much better."*
>
> **Michael Jordan**

PRIME SKI RACING PYRAMID

This book is directed toward helping you experience the feeling and performances of Prime Ski Racing. This goal is accomplished by ascending the Prime Ski Racing pyramid, which is comprised of five essential mental factors that impact race performance: motivation, confidence, intensity, focus, and emotions (see page 15). By developing these mental areas, you will achieve Prime Ski Racing.

These five mental factors are ordered in a way that each area builds on the previous ones leading to Prime Ski Racing. At the base of the Prime Ski Racing pyramid lies motivation because without motivation there is no interest or desire to train. Prime motivation ensures that you put in the necessary time and effort to be totally prepared to ski your best. From motivation and preparation comes confidence in your physical, technical, and tactical capabilities, and in your ability to ski your best. Prime confidence gives you the desire to compete and the belief that you can win. From confidence comes the ability to manage your intensity and respond positively to the pressures of competition. Prime intensity enables you to consistently maintain your ideal level of intensity so you are physically capable of skiing your best. From intensity comes the ability to focus properly during training and competition. Prime focus lets you stay focused and avoid distractions. From these four mental factors comes the ability to master your emotions. Prime emotions ensure that your emotions help rather than hurt your racing performances and that you are your best ally instead of your worst enemy while competing. Having ascended the Prime Ski Racing pyramid, you will have the tools to achieve Prime Ski Racing.

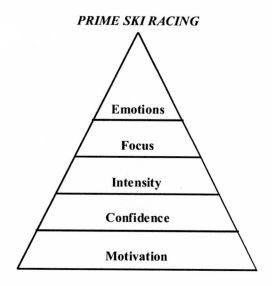

PRIME SKI RACING

SECTION II

PRIME SKI RACING ASSESSMENT

CHAPTER ONE:

PRIME SKI RACING PROFILING

Now that you have an understanding of Prime Ski Racing, you can begin the process of achieving it. The first step involves gaining a better understanding of yourself as a ski racer. Self-understanding is so important because it shows you your strengths and areas in need of improvement and enables you to realize how you react in certain situations. This self-understanding then results in more efficient change. Becoming the best ski racer you can is complicated. You probably have a busy life filled with ski racing, other sports, school, work, family, social life, and other activities. It's difficult to find time to do everything. By understanding yourself, you'll know what you need to work on to be efficient and focused in your efforts.

In developing greater self-understanding, racers must recognize their strengths and weaknesses. Most racers love to focus on their strengths, but don't like to admit that they have weaknesses. This attitude will limit their development. Most racers think that they're as good as their greatest strengths. The truth is, however, that racers are only as good as their biggest weakness. For example, a racer may be very good on the steeps because he has power and agility. But it is his lack of ability to glide on the flats that will keep him from realizing his full ability. Herman Maier saw that, though his strength and risk-taking has allowed him to achieve considerable successful, he lacked the agility and touch to be consistently successful on highly technical courses. So, during the summer of 1999, he trained with the Austrian technical team and refined his technique and feel for the snow. The following year he was more dominant than ever before.

Think of ski racing strengths and weaknesses as a mathematical equation (see Prime Profile Formula below). If a downhiller is a good glider (8), but she is not fast on steep, icy courses (2), her overall performances would be low (8+2=10). If she worked on and improved your skiing on the steeps (7), then her overall performances would rise significantly (8+7=15). The more racers improve their weaknesses, the higher their overall performances will be and the more they will win.

PRIME PROFILE FORMULA

Strengths + Weaknesses = Overall Ski Racing Performance

WHY PRIME SKI RACING PROFILING?

A difficulty with dealing with the mental aspects of ski racing is that they're not tangible or easily measured. If you want to learn what are your physical strengths and weaknesses, you can go through a physical testing program that gives you objective data about your physical condition. Think of Prime Ski Racing profiling as physical testing for the mind. It makes mental issues related to ski racing more concrete. Prime Ski Racing profiling increases your self-understanding so you can take active steps to maintain your strengths and improve your weaknesses.

It's important for you to have an open mind with Prime Ski Racing profiling. Rather than being uncomfortable with facing your weaknesses, you should be willing to consider the information in a positive and constructive way. When weaknesses are identified, it doesn't mean that you're incapable of skiing well. It may be that you haven't had to use these skills at your current level or you've been able to hide them with the strengths you have.

"As you grow up, you learn more about yourself, I tried to...learn about myself and my weaknesses and strengths."

Olympic champion Lasse Kjus

COMPLETING THE PRIME SKI RACING PROFILE

The Prime Ski Racing profile (see page 24) is comprised of 12 mental, emotional, and competitive factors that impact race performance. To complete the Prime Ski Racing profile, read the description of each factor and rate yourself on a one-to-ten scale by drawing a line at that level and shading in the area toward the center of the profile.

Motivation refers to how determined you are to train and compete to achieve your ski racing goals. Motivation affects all aspects of your preparation including your desire to put time and energy into physical conditioning, technical and tactical development, and mental preparation. Do you work consistently hard on all aspects of your ski racing or do you give up when you get tired, bored, or frustrated? (1-not at all motivated; 10-very motivated)

Confidence relates to how positive or negative your self-talk and body language are before races. It includes how well you're able to maintain your confidence between runs, especially after a poor first run. Do you stay positive even under pressure and when you're not skiing well or do you become negative and get down on yourself? (1-very negative; 10-very positive)

Intensity involves whether your physical intensity helps or hurts your racing. In pressure situations, are you able to maintain a level of intensity that allows you to ski well or do you become too anxious to ski well? (1-hurts, anxious; 10-helps, just right)

Focus is concerned with how well you're able to keep your mind on skiing your best before and during races. It involves avoiding distractions and not losing focus in difficult races. Are you able to stay focused on what you need to in order to ski well or do you become distracted by things that hurt your racing? (1-distracted; 10-focused)

Emotions involve how well you're able to control your emotions before races and between runs. Particularly in difficult races or when you're not skiing well, do you stay positive and excited or do you get frustrated, angry, or depressed? Simply put, do your emotions help or hurt you during races? (1-lose control, hurt; 10-have control, help)

Consistency relates to how well you're able to maintain your level of performance during a race. Does your level of skiing stay at a consistently high level or does it go up and down frequently during a race? (1-very inconsistent; 10-very consistent)

Routines involve how much you use routines in your ski racing. Do you have a pre-race routine to prepare for race? Do you have a routine between runs? How consistent are you in using routines in your racing? (1-never; 10-often)

Competitor refers to how well you ski in races as compared to training. Do you ski better, the same, or worse in races as compared to training? (1-not as well; 10-better)

Adversity is concerned with your ability to respond positively to difficulties you're faced with during races. For example, how do you react when the conditions are poor or your competition is tough? (1-poorly; 10-well)

Pressure relates to your ability to ski your best in difficult race situations such as when you are ahead after the first run. Does your skiing decline or improve when the race is on the line? (1-decline; 10-improve)

Ally involves whether you are your best ally or your worst enemy during a race. Are you positive and encouraging to yourself or do you get angry and berate yourself, especially when you're behind after the first run or not skiing well? (1-enemy; 10-ally)

Prime Ski Racing refers to how often you achieve and maintain your highest level of racing. Are you able to achieve Prime Ski Racing regularly or is it a rare occurrence for you? (1-never; 10-often)

PRIME SKI RACING PROFILE

Name _____   **Date** _____

Directions: Twelve mental factors that impact ski racing are identified in the profile below. Using the definitions provided above, rate yourself on a 1-10 scale for each factor by drawing a line at that level and shading in the area toward the center of profile. A score below a *7* indicates an area in need of improvement.

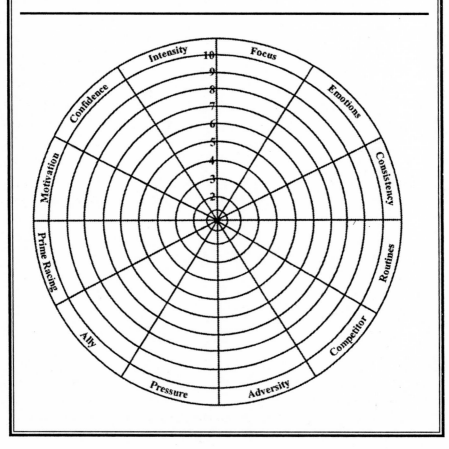

USING YOUR PRIME SKI RACING PROFILE

Having completed the Prime Ski Racing profile, you now have a clear picture of what you believe to be the mental strengths and weaknesses in your ski racing. Typically, a score below a 7 indicates an area on which you need to work. Place a ✓ next to each factor that you scored as less than a 7. These are the factors that you'll want to consider working on in your Prime Ski Racing program.

From those checked factors, select three to focus on in the immediate future. It doesn't make sense to deal with every one that you need to strengthen. You'll just become overloaded and won't give adequate attention to any of them. It's best to focus on a few, strengthen them, then move on to others.

The question is, if you have more than three factors on which you need to work, which ones should you choose? The decision should be based on several concerns. First, you should look at which ones are most important for your long-term development. Just like working on the physical and technical aspects of your skiing, you should focus on the factors that will help you in the long run. Second, some weaknesses are symptoms of other weaknesses. By dealing with one factor, another one can be relieved without having to work on it directly. For example, you may not handle pressure well because you lack confidence. By building your confidence, you also improve your ability to handle pressure. Third, you need to balance your immediate training and competitive needs with your long-term development. You may have an important race coming up for which you need to be ready. For example, you may decide that you need to improve your focus and intensity immediately even though working on your motivation and confidence will be more important in the future.

Using the Prime Ski Racing Priority form (see page 27), indicate the three mental factors you want to focus on in the near future. After reading *Prime Ski Racing*, return to the relevant chapters to learn about techniques and exercises that will help you strengthen the areas you've selected. Use the goal setting and Prime Ski Racing program described in Section V to work on those areas.

You can also use Prime Ski Racing Profiling to measure progress in your training. Periodically, perhaps once a month, complete the profile and compare it with your past profiles. You should see improvement in the areas on which you've worked. Also, ask your coaches about positive changes they've seen in those areas. When your ratings move above 7, select other factors to work on and follow the same procedure.

> *"A part of greatness is learning to correct your weaknesses. The first thing is to know your faults and then take on a systematic plan of correcting them."*
>
> **Babe Ruth**

PRIME SKI RACING PRIORITY

Name _____   **Date** _____

Directions: In the space below, indicate three areas that you have identified in your Prime Ski Racing profile on which you would like to focus. As these areas improve and new areas need work, complete this form again to specify the new priorities.

1.

2.

3.

SECTION III

PRIME SKI RACING PYRAMID

CHAPTER TWO:

MOTIVATION

Motivation lies at the base of the Prime Ski Racing pyramid. Without the desire and determination to improve your racing, all of the other mental factors, confidence, intensity, focus, and emotions, are meaningless. To become the best racer you can be, you must be motivated to do what it takes to maximize your ability.

Motivation, simply defined, is the ability to initiate and persist at a task. To ski your best, you must want to begin the process of developing as a racer and you must be willing to maintain your efforts until you have achieved your goals. Motivation in ski racing is so important because you must be willing to work hard in the face of fatigue, boredom, pain, cold, and the desire to do other things. Motivation will impact everything that influences ski racing: physical conditioning, technical and tactical training, mental preparation, and general lifestyle including sleep, diet, school or work, and relationships.

The reason motivation is so important is that it is the only contributor to ski racing over which you have control. My Performance Formula (see below) helps explain this notion. There are three things that affect how well you ski. First, your ability, which includes your physical, technical, tactical, and mental capabilities, impacts your level of performance. Though these four factors can change over time with training, on any given day, you can not alter them dramatically. For example, a racer is not going to significantly improve her line during warm-up runs before a race. Whatever you bring to the race in terms of your ability is what you will have to use that day. In the short-run, you have little real control over your ability.

PERFORMANCE FORMULA

Ability - Difficulty of Race + Motivation = PERFORMANCE

Second, the difficulty of the race influences performance. Contributors to difficulty include the level of competition and external factors such as weather and snow conditions. You have no control over these factors.

Finally, motivation will impact race performance. Motivation will directly affect your long-term development and the level that you ultimately achieve. If you're highly motivated to improve your racing, then you will put in the time and effort necessary to improve your skiing. Motivation will also influence how you ski in races. If you're competing against a field of nearly equal skill, it will not be ability that will determine the outcome. Rather, it will be the racers who work the hardest, who don't give up, and who ski their best when it counts. In other words, the racers who are most motivated to win will be the most successful.

> *"Testing, taxing, bruising, beating, striving, driving, sweating; it's the hard work and the hard falls that make each hard won victory a precious experience of satisfaction and exaltation worth living for."*
>
> **Former USST member Becky Dorsey**

SIGNS OF LOW MOTIVATION

Two questions you must ask yourself are, "How motivated am I?" and "Am I as motivated as I can be?" There are some common signs of low motivation. A lack of desire to train as much as you could is one clear symptom of low motivation. This is especially important if your goals are high. Goals are great to have, but they will be unfulfilled if you are not motivated to achieve them. It's very important that motivation be consistent with goals. Are you willing to do what is necessary to reach your goals? If not, then you have two choices: increase your motivation so you can attain your goals or lower your goals to a level that, given your motivation, you will be able to reach.

Less than 100% effort in training is another warning sign of low motivation. When you train, do you give it your all? Do you work as hard as you can when you're training? Or do you not try that hard and put less than complete effort into your training? Skipping or shortening training sessions is also common for racers with low motivation. If racers are not motivated, it's easy to skip training because they just don't feel like it. If they do go to training, they may only stay for a little while or they may goof around more than they train. If you exhibit any of these symptoms of low motivation, you're not going to be the best ski racer you can be. If you're not as motivated as you could be, you have to do two things. First, ask yourself why you're not working as hard as you could. Second, you must take active steps to increase your motivation in your ski racing.

> *"You've got to care. You start uncovering the layers of everything surrounding the game—the money, the hype, the stardom—and it comes down to this: How bad do you want it?"*
>
> **NFL player Carnell Lake**

PRIME MOTIVATION

Prime motivation means putting 100% of your time, effort, energy, and focus into all aspects of your ski racing. It involves doing everything possible to become the best racer you can be. Prime motivation is based on what I call the three D's (see below). The first D stands for *direction*. Before you can attain prime motivation, you must first consider the different directions you can go in your ski racing. You have three choices: stop racing completely, continue at your current level, or strive to be the best racer you can be.

The second D represents *decision*. With these three choices of direction, you must select one direction in which to go. None of these directions are necessarily right or wrong, better or worse, they're simply your options. Your choice will dictate the amount of time and effort you will put into your ski racing and how good a racer you will ultimately become.

The third D stands for *dedication*. Once you've made your decision, you must dedicate yourself to it. If your decision is to become the best racer you can be, then this last step, dedication, will determine whether you have prime motivation. Your decision to be your best and your dedication to your ski racing must be a top priority. Only by being completely dedicated to your direction and decision will you ensure that you have prime motivation.

THREE D'S

Direction → Decision → Dedication → MOTIVATION

DEVELOPING PRIME MOTIVATION

Focus on your long-term goals. To be your best, you have to put a lot of time and effort into your ski racing. But all of that time and effort is not always enjoyable. I call this the *Grind*, which involves having to put hours upon hours of time into training, well beyond the point that it is fun and exciting. If you let these immediate negative aspects of ski racing override the long-term benefits of working hard and putting in the time, your motivation is going to suffer and you're not going to get the most out of your ski racing.

During those times when you're in the Grind and your motivation is suffering, focus on your long-term goals. Remind yourself why you're working so hard. Imagine exactly what you want to accomplish and tell yourself that the only way you'll be able to reach your goals is to go through the Grind. Also, try to generate the feelings of joy and fulfillment that you will experience when you reach your goals. This technique will distract you from the unpleasantness of the Grind, focus you on what you want to achieve, and generate positive thoughts and emotions that will get you through the Grind.

Have a training partner. It's difficult to be highly motivated all of the time on your own. There are going to be some days when you don't feel like getting out there. Also, no matter how hard you push yourself, you will work that much harder if you have someone pushing you. The best person to have is a regular training partner. A training partner is someone at about your level of ability and with similar goals. You can work together to accomplish your goals. The chances are on any given day that one of you will be motivated. Even if you're not very psyched to train on a particular day, you will still put in the time and effort because your partner is counting on you.

Focus on greatest competitor. Another way to keep yourself motivated is to focus on your greatest competitor. I have racers identify who their biggest competition is and put his or her name or photo where they can see it every day. Ask yourself, "Am I working as hard as him/her?" Remember that only by working your hardest will you have a chance to overcome your greatest competitor.

Motivational cues. A big part of staying motivated involves generating positive emotions associated with your efforts and achieving your goals. A way to keep those feelings is with motivational cues such as inspirational phrases and photographs. If you come across a quote or a picture that moves you, place it where you can see it regularly such as in your bedroom, on your refrigerator door, or in your locker. Look at it periodically and allow yourself to experience the emotions it creates in you. These reminders and the emotions associated with them will inspire and motivate you to work hard in your ski racing.

Set goals. There are few things more rewarding and motivating than setting a goal, putting effort toward the goal, and achieving the goal. The sense of accomplishment and validation of the effort makes you feel good and motivates you to strive higher. It's valuable to establish clear goals of what you want to accomplish in your ski racing and how you will achieve those goals. Section V will describe how to do just that. Seeing that your hard work leads to progress and results should motivate you further to realize your ski racing goals.

Daily questions. Every day, you should ask yourself two questions. When you get up in the morning, ask, "What can I do today to become the best ski racer I can be?" and before you go to sleep, ask, "Did I do everything possible today to become the best ski racer I can be?" These two questions will remind you daily of what your goal is and will challenge you to be motivated to become your best.

The heart of motivation. A final point about motivation. The techniques I've just described are effective in increasing your motivation. Motivation, though, is not something that can be given to you. Rather, motivation must ultimately come from within. You must simply want to ski race. Motivation won't be a problem if you race for the right reasons.

There are two things that should motivate you to race. First, you should compete because you have a great passion for ski racing. If you love ski racing, you will be motivated to ski to best of your ability.

Second, you should race because you love the process. Not the winning, not the trophies, not the rankings, though they can certainly make you feel good. You should race because you just love to get out there and do it. There are not many World Cup racers who don't love the Grind. It is that love that helps make them successful. If you truly love to ski race, your motivation to work at all aspects of ski racing will be high.

"Training to win takes competitive drive."

USST member Sarah Schleper

TWELVE LAWS OF PRIME PREPARATION

By achieving prime motivation, you take the first and most crucial step toward reaching your ski racing goals. You can now follow what I call the Prime Motivation Progression (see below). Prime motivation pushes you to put in the necessary time and effort to be the best ski racer you can be. This time and effort ensures that you have prime preparation, which I define as doing everything you can to be fully prepared to ski your best.

PRIME MOTIVATION PROGRESSION

Prime Motivation → Prime Preparation → Prime Ski Racing

It is preparation that acts as the bridge between prime motivation and Prime Ski Racing. Without preparation, you will not have the tools or the experience to achieve your ski racing goals. From my years of working with racers at all levels of ability, I have developed twelve laws that must be understood and followed in order to accomplish prime preparation and achieve Prime Ski Racing.

First Law: *Races are not won on the day you race, but rather in the days, weeks, and months before the race.* Many racers believe that if they're ready to go on the day of a race, then they will be prepared to ski their best. But I have found that success is determined more by what you do in the days, weeks, and months leading up to the race. If you've put in the time and effort to develop your physical, technical, tactical, and mental abilities, you will have the skills and the belief to ski your best on race day.

Second Law: *Take responsibility for everything that can impact your ski racing.* The only way that prime preparation can be achieved is if you know every area that influences your ski racing performances. These areas include all of the components of physical, technical, tactical, and mental preparation. If you address every one of these areas, you can be sure that when you get to the race, you will be totally prepared to ski your best.

Third Law: *Preparation is the foundation of all physical, technical, tactical, and mental skills.* There is no magic to acquiring skills. There are no special techniques that enable you to learn faster or better. Developing skills of any sort requires three steps: (1) Awareness of what you're doing incorrectly and what is the proper execution; (2) Control to engage in the skills correctly; and (3) Repetition to ingrain the new skills. Only with this preparation will you be able to use those skills effectively and with confidence in a race.

Fourth Law: *The purpose of training is to develop effective skills and habits.* Training will ingrain in you a variety of physical, technical, tactical, and mental skills. If you want to experience Prime Ski Racing, you must be sure that you're developing skills and habits that will facilitate rather than interfere with Prime Ski Racing. Whatever you practice, those are the skills and habits that you will learn. If you practice effective skills and habits, you'll develop skills and habits that will help you ski your best. If you practice poor skills and habits, you'll become good at those and they will hurt your skiing. You will become highly skilled at ineffective skills. It's important that you're always practicing physical, technical, tactical, and mental skills that will allow you to achieve Prime Ski Racing.

Fifth Law: *Racers should train like they race.* Whenever I give a seminar to racers or coaches, I ask this question: Should you train like you race or should you race like you train? Most people say, you should race like you train. Their response is understandable in some ways because if you could race in the positive, relaxed, and focused way that you train, then you would certainly ski well. I believe that racing like you train is impossible for one simple reason: racing matters. Training is easy because you don't care that much how you ski. If you ski poorly in races, though, you do care.

The problem is that many ski racers train at 60-70%, then expect to be able to jump to 100% motivation, focus, and intensity and ski their best. Unfortunately, this leap is too great and they ski poorly. Training like you race means putting as close to the same level of motivation, focus, and intensity into training as you do in a race. It's probably unrealistic to think that you can train exactly like you race. If you can get close to it, say 90%, then the last 10% that comes in a race will be an easy step up.

Sixth Law: *Prime preparation requires clear purpose, prime focus, and prime intensity*. It's impossible to engage in quality training unless three things are present. You must have a clear purpose that tells you what you're working on. If you don't know what you're doing to improve, you won't be able to do it. Identifying the purpose of your preparation ensures that you put directed effort into that purpose.

You must have prime focus which involves consistently maintaining focus on your purpose and avoiding distractions that will interfere with that focus. This means having cues to focus on that remind you of your purpose and ways of redirecting your focus when you become distracted.

You must have prime intensity to achieve prime preparation. All of the mental techniques in the world won't work if your body is not prepared to execute the purpose you have identified. Having the awareness and control of your intensity will enable your body to ingrain the purpose and focus that you have worked on.

Seventh Law: *Consistent training leads to consistent ski racing*. Consistency is essential to Prime Ski Racing and is one of the most important qualities that put the best racers above the rest. The consistency in Prime Ski Racing comes from consistency in training. Referring back to my fourth law, consistency is one of those effective skills and habits that you need to develop in order to achieve Prime Ski Racing. Consistency relates to every aspect of race training and life. In addition to the obvious areas such as conditioning, technique, and tactics, it also pertains to areas including attitude, effort, focus, intensity, emotions, sleep, and diet. Any area that influences your ski racing needs to be consistent before your skiing can be consistent.

Eighth Law: *Patience and persistence are essential to achieving Prime Tennis*. Skills take time to develop and you will experience plateaus, setbacks, and obstacles along the path toward Prime Ski Racing. You may get frustrated, impatient, and want to quit. If you let frustration and impatience overwhelm you, you will never achieve Prime Ski Racing. If you understand that progress takes time and that there is no way to hurry the learning process, you will have the patience to allow yourself to experience Prime Ski Racing. Drawing on that patience, if you persist long enough in the face of the setbacks and obstacles, the improvement will come and you will achieve Prime Ski Racing.

Ninth Law: *Failure is necessary for Prime Ski Racing*. Many ski racers believe that failure, in the form of mistakes, poor finishes, or DNF's, is something to be avoided. If you fail, then you're a failure. If you fail, then you will never be successful. But there can not be success without failure. Failure shows you what is not working. It means that you are moving out of your comfort zone. Failure means you are taking risks. Failure teaches you how to deal positively with adversity.

Tenth Law: *Prime Ski Racing comes from "one more thing, one more time."* You can assume that most of your competitors are working hard to become the best ski racers they can be. If you want to defeat them, you must ask yourself, "What can I do to get the edge over them?" Here is a simple rule I learned from Bernhard Russi, 1972 Olympic downhill champion: "One more thing, one more time." When you feel you have done enough, you should take one more training run, do one more set of weights, or do another wind sprint. By doing one more thing, one more time, you are doing that little bit extra that would separate you on the day of the race.

Eleventh Law: *It takes 10 years and 10,000 hours to become a great ski racer.* Research that has looked at expert performance in sports, music, chess, and other areas found two things that predict the level that someone will achieve: how long they've been committed to the activity and how much they trained. Applied to ski racing, the longer you have skied and the more hours you have trained, the better you will be.

Twelfth Law: *Prime preparation is devoted to readying racers to ski their best under the most demanding conditions in the most important races of their lives.* I'm not interested in you skiing well in an unimportant race, under ideal conditions, against a field that you know you can defeat. The ultimate goal of Prime Ski Racing is for you to ski your best when it really matters. Prime preparation will allow you to achieve Prime Ski Racing in your equivalent of the Olympics, the World Championships, or the World Cup.

> *"Preparation is everything to winning. It is easy to say, 'I am going to win.' So I don't think about it; instead I concentrate on my training...which really determines who will make it. Then, on the day of the race...I can say with confidence, 'I am ready.'"*

Olympic champion Jean-Claude Killy

CHAPTER THREE:

CONFIDENCE

Confidence is the single most important mental factor for success in ski racing. I define confidence as how strongly you believe you can ski your best. Confidence impacts two levels of your ski racing: your ability to ski your best and your ability to win. Confidence is so important because you may have all of the ability in the world to ski well, but if you don't believe you have that ability, then you won't ski up to that ability. For example, a racer may have the ability to ski a straighter line in slalom, but if she doesn't believe she can hold that line for an entire run, she won't try to ski that line at all.

Have you ever seen racers who compete at a high level, but are not considered among the best? For example, there are racers who are successful in Nor-Ams and Europa Cups, but can't quite make it on the World Cup. What you see are outstanding racers with exceptional skills in most facets of ski racing. What separates these racers from those who are in the top two seeds in the world if they seem to have similar skills at their disposal? It is often not their physical or technical capabilities but rather their belief in their ability to ski their best in the most important races of their lives. The best racers have the confidence that they will ski their best and be successful when it really counts. The lower-ranked racers don't have that confidence, so they won't go quite as hard or take the necessary risks to succeed at the highest level.

Too often racers are their own worst enemy rather than their best ally. Whether you're your best ally or your worst enemy depends on your confidence. If you don't have much confidence in yourself, you probably don't think you can ski your best and win. If that's the case and your competition has confidence, then you're in an impossible situation. As your worst enemy, your competition is against you and you are against you. The only way you have the chance to win is to become your best ally. You have to allow yourself to be on your own side. Only then will you have any chance of skiing well and winning.

> *"I have no secret. I just feel very confident, and that allows me to take all the risks I want and to push all the way down the hill."*
>
> **World Cup GS champion Michael Von Greunigen**

VICIOUS CYCLE OR UPWARD SPIRAL

Not only does confidence impact your ski racing directly, it also affects every other mental factor. To help illustrate this influence of confidence, think back to a time when you didn't have confidence in your racing. You probably got caught in a vicious cycle of low confidence and performance in which negative thinking led to poor performance, which led to more negative thinking and even poorer performance, until your confidence was so low that you didn't even want to race (see page 48).

This vicious cycle usually starts with a period of poor results. These poor results can lead to negative thinking and self-talk. "I'm terrible. I can't do this. I don't have a chance. I can't ski well today." You are becoming your own worst enemy.

You start to get nervous before a race because you believe you will ski poorly. All of that anxiety hurts your confidence even more because you feel physically uncomfortable and there's no way you can ski well when you're so uptight. The negative self-talk and anxiety cause negative emotions. You feel frustrated, angry, depressed, and helpless, all of which hurt your confidence more and cause you to ski even worse.

The negative self-talk, anxiety, and emotions then hurt your focus. If you have low confidence, you can't help but focus on all of the negative things rather than on things that will enable you to ski your best. All of this accumulated negativity hurts your motivation. As bad as you feel, you just want to get out of there. If you're thinking negatively, caught in a vicious cycle, feeling nervous and frustrated, and can't focus, you're not going to have much fun and you're not going to ski well.

In contrast to those times when you have had low confidence, recall when you have been really confident. Your self-talk is positive. "I'm a good ski racer. I can ski well. I can win." Instead of being your worst enemy, you're your best ally.

With the positive self-talk, rather than being dragged down into the vicious cycle, you begin an upward spiral of high confidence and skiing in which positive thinking leads to better skiing, which leads to more positive thinking and even better skiing (see page 48).

All of the positive talk gets you feeling relaxed and energized before the race. You have a lot of positive emotions such as happiness, joy and excitement. You focus on things you need to ski your best. Racing is actually an enjoyable experience for you.

All of the positive thoughts and feelings motivate you to race. If you're thinking positively, riding an upward spiral, feeling relaxed and energized, experiencing happiness and excitement, and are focused on skiing your best, you're going to have a lot of fun and you're going to ski well.

"If you're not skiing well, you'll definitely be down on yourself. But you can't really ride low in the slumps; you have to dig yourself out as quickly as possible."

Former USST member Monique Pelletier

WHY RACERS LOSE CONFIDENCE

Remember that confidence is the belief racers have in their ability to ski well. Anything that counters that belief will hurt their confidence. The most disruptive thing to hurt confidence is failure of any kind. Failure can mean making mistakes or falling in races, for example, sliding low on a turn or hooking a tip. Failure will cause racers to lose confidence in themselves and cause them to become tentative or cautious in their skiing. Failure can also mean having had poor results in recent races. Racers who have skied poorly may question their ability to ski fast and may become unwilling to take risks and ski all out.

Unrealistic expectations can also hurt confidence. You should make sure that your confidence is realistic. In other words, is your confidence in your ability consistent with your actual ability? If it is not, then you'll have unrealistic expectations that can never be reached. You may be overly critical of your skiing based on those unreasonable beliefs about your ability, believing that you didn't ski as well as you should have instead of simply having skied up to your realistic ability.

Lack of experience or skills can also hurt confidence. If you have not competed very much or have not raced at the current level in which you're now competing, you may not have the experience to adequately evaluate how well you should ski. Often, results that are interpreted as poor are actually just the level of competition being higher. This is particularly likely if you're racing at a new level above where you had previously competed. You may simply lack the experience to be competitive at that level yet. Without this realization, instead of adjusting your perceptions accordingly, you'll assume that you're skiing poorly and your confidence will decline.

> *"It's when you don't know what's going to happen, when you're not confident on your skis, not confident of your line, or how you will adapt your line at certain speeds—then that's when you want to go and hide."*

> **Casey Puckett**

CONFIDENCE IS A SKILL

A misconception that many racers have is that confidence is something that is inborn or that if they don't have it at an early age, they will never have confidence. In reality, confidence is a skill, much like technical skills, that can be learned. Just like with any type of skill, confidence is developed through practice and experience.

The problem many racers have with confidence is that they violate my fourth law of preparation. They developed ineffective confidence skills and habits, and by practicing being negative, they became skilled at being negative. These racers became highly skilled at something that actually hurts their skiing.

If a racer has a bad technical habit, for example, she drops her hands in slalom, she probably has trained that way for a long time. She has become skilled at dropping her hands. The same holds true for confidence. Racers can become skilled at being negative.

To change bad confidence skills, racers must retrain the way they think. They have to practice good confidence skills regularly until the old negative habits have been broken and they have learned and ingrained the new positive skills of confidence. The techniques described below will help you in this process by giving you specific strategies you can use to unlearn bad habits and learn good skills.

A question I'm often asked is, "Do you become confident by succeeding or do you succeed from being confident?" I believe that success in ski racing comes from confidence. You don't just go from 0% confidence to 100% confidence in one big step. Rather, it's a building process in which confidence leads to success which reinforces the confidence which, in turn, leads to more success. For example, a racer may only have 40% confidence in his ability to consistently finish GS races. By working on his technique and his physical conditioning and using the confidence-building techniques described on the following pages, his confidence goes up to 60%. Yet, all of the positive thinking in the world won't help if he doesn't have experiences to confirm his beliefs. With his confidence now at 60%, the racer is able to have greater focus and intensity in his training, which results in improved technique and more consistency in his training runs. His hard work and progress raise his confidence to 80%. His improved preparation and greater confidence results in more consistency in his GS training runs. His improved consistency and his success in training then increases his confidence to near 100%, enabling him to achieve greater consistency and success in his GS races.

"You have to believe in the start but you can win. It's a question of attitude."

Austrian World Cup racer Benjamin Raich

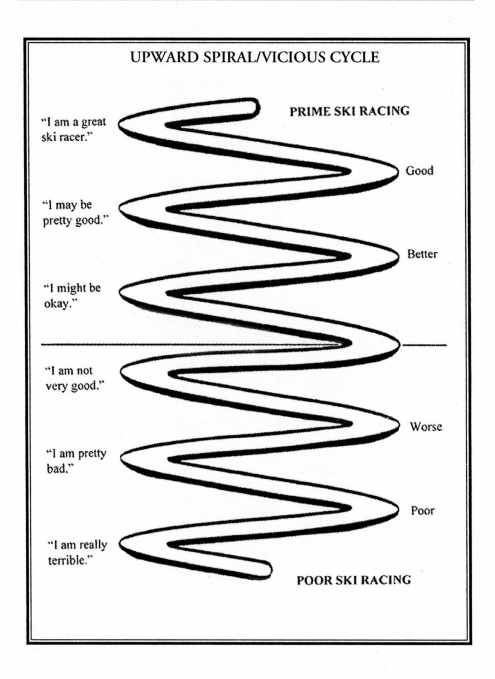

PRIME CONFIDENCE

Prime confidence is a deep, lasting, and resilient belief in one's ability. With prime confidence, racers are able to stay confident even when they're not skiing well. Prime confidence keeps racers positive, motivated, intense, focused, and emotionally in control when they need to be. Racers are not negative and uncertain in difficult races and they're not overconfident in easy races. It also encourages racers to seek out pressure situations and to view difficult conditions and tough opponents as challenges to pursue. Prime confidence enables racers to ski at their highest level consistently.

Prime confidence is a belief, not a certainty, that racers can win. It is the confidence that if racers do the right things, they will prevail. Prime confidence demonstrates faith and trust in their ability and their preparation. It does not, however, lead racers to know, expect, or have to win. This belief can produce arrogance and overconfidence. It can also cause racers to become too focused on winning the race instead of skiing their best in the race. This perception can lead to self-imposed pressure and a fear of losing.

> *"Developing confidence was what finally enabled me to win an Olympic gold medal."*
>
> **Jean-Claude Killy**

PROGRESSION OF CONFIDENCE

I have identified a four-step progression that will lead you along the upward spiral of confidence. Each step alone can enhance your confidence, but if you use all of them together, you'll find your confidence growing stronger and more quickly. The ultimate goal of prime confidence is to develop a strong and resilient belief in your skiing ability so that you have the confidence to give your best effort, ski at your highest level, and believe you can be successful in the most important races of your life.

Preparation breeds confidence. Preparation is the foundation of confidence. If you believe that you have done everything you can to ski your best, you will have confidence in your ability to ski well. This preparation includes the physical, technical, tactical, and mental parts of ski racing. If you have developed these areas as fully as you can, you will have faith that you will be able to use those skills gained from preparation to ski as well as you can. The more of these areas you cover in your preparation, the more confidence you will breed in yourself.

Mental skills reinforce confidence. As I have indicated previously, confidence is a skill that develops with practice. A meaningful way to strengthen the confidence you've built through preparation is to use mental skills that provide repetition of the confidence. These mental skills include goal setting to bolster motivation, positive self-talk and body language to fortify the confident beliefs, intensity control to combat confidence-depleting anxiety, keywords to maintain focus and avoid distractions, and emotional control to stay calm under pressure. These mental skills are described throughout Section III.

Adversity ingrains confidence. It's one thing to be confident when you're skiing well and things are going your way. It is an entirely different challenge to maintain your belief in yourself when you're faced with adversity. To more deeply ingrain confidence in your skiing, you should expose yourself to as much adversity as possible. Adversity can involve anything that takes you out of your comfort zone. Adversity can include bad weather, poor snow conditions, or a race hill on which you have never skied well. Adversity can also involve racing in a higher level race in which the competition is better.

Skiing under adversity has several essential benefits. It demonstrates your competence to ski well under difficult conditions. Adversity teaches you additional skills you can use to ski at a higher level. It also prepares you for adversity that you will inevitably experience when you ski in important races. All of these aspects of adversity will ingrain confidence in your ski racing.

Success validates confidence. All of the previous steps in building confidence would go for naught if you did not then ski well and have success in races. Success validates the confidence you have developed in your ability. It demonstrates that your belief in your ability is well-founded. Success further strengthens your confidence, making it more resilient in the face of adversity and poor races. Finally, success rewards your efforts to build confidence, encouraging you to continue to work hard and develop your skiing.

> *"Confidence comes from laying the strong foundation to build a career on: physical conditioning, eating a well balance diet, getting plenty of rest, having the right equipment to fit your needs, and having a well thought out long range plan. Confidence comes from hard work and making sacrifices."*
>
> **Former U.S. Olympic ski coach Finn Gundersen**

BUILDING PRIME CONFIDENCE

You now see the importance of having prime confidence. Let's discuss how you can develop your confidence with Prime Ski Racing techniques. One mistake that racers often make is they wait to do mental training until after they've lost confidence. You don't wait to get hurt before you start doing physical training. You don't wait to develop a technical problem before you work on technique. You do them beforehand to prevent the problems. The same thing holds true for building confidence.

Walk the walk. One thing I've noticed about working with world-class racers is that they carry themselves a certain way. They move and walk with confidence. A first step in developing confidence is to learn to "walk the walk." How you carry yourself, move, and walk affects what you think and how you feel. If your body is down, your thoughts and feelings will be negative. If your body is up, your thoughts and feelings will be positive. It's hard to feel down when your body is up. Walking the walk involves moving with your head high, chin up, eyes forward, shoulders back, arms swinging, and a bounce in your step. You look and move like a winner.

In contrast, not walking the walk involves your head, eyes, and shoulders down, feet dragging, and no energy in your step. You look and move like a loser. To give you a feeling of what this is like, try walking the walk and saying negative things about yourself. As you will see, it's difficult to do because your thoughts are inconsistent with what your body is signaling to you. Then try not walking the walk and saying positive things. Again, it's difficult because your thoughts conflict with what your body is doing.

Related to walking the walk, you can influence your thoughts and feelings with your body language. To get more positive, clench your fist, pump your arms, slap your thigh. This positive body language will affect your thinking and emotions, especially if you combine it with high-energy positive self-talk.

Talk the talk. In addition to walking the walk, you can also learn to "talk the talk." What you say to yourself affects what you think and how you feel. If your talk is negative, your thoughts and feelings will be negative. If your talk is positive, your thoughts and feelings will be positive. It's hard to think and feel negative when you're talking positively. Don't say, "I don't have a chance today." Say, "I'm going to try my hardest today. I'm going to ski the best I can." That will get you positive and fired up. By talking the talk, you're also being your own best ally. You're showing yourself that your competition may be against you, but you're on your side.

Conversely, not talking the talk includes "I'm going to ski terribly today," "I may do okay," and "I don't know how I'll do today." If you say these things to yourself, you're convincing yourself that you have little chance. With that attitude, you really have no chance because not only is your competition planning on defeating you, but you're planning on losing to them as well.

Balance the scales. When I work with racers, I always chart the number of positive and negative things they say or do before a race. In most cases, the negatives far outnumber the positives. In an ideal world, I would love to eliminate all negatives and have racers only express positives. But this is the real world and any racer who cares about ski racing is going to feel and express frustration, anger, and despair occasionally.

In dealing with this reality, you should learn to *balance the scales*. If you're going to be negative when you make mistakes and ski poorly, you should also be positive when you ski well. The immediate goal is to increase the positives. This means rewarding yourself when you ski well. If you beat yourself up over a mistake or a DNF, why shouldn't you pat yourself on the back when you get it right. Pump your fist, slap your leg, say, "yes," when you ski well. It will psych you up and make you feel positive and excited.

Once you've balanced the scales by increasing your positives, your next goal is to tip the scales in the positive direction by reducing the negatives. Ask why you're so hard on yourself when you ski poorly. The best racers in the world don't always ski their best. Why shouldn't it be okay for you to have down periods in your racing?

Become aware of your negative self-talk and body language. Do things that counter the negativity. For example, after you make a mistake in a course, instead of dropping your head and saying, "I stink," try picking your head up and saying, "Come on!"

This step of tipping the scales toward positives is so important because of some recent research that found that negative experiences such as negative self-talk, negative body language, and negative emotions carry more weight than positive experiences. In fact, it takes 12 positive experiences to equal one negative experience. What this means is that for every negative expression you make, whether saying something negative or screaming in frustration, you must express yourself positively 12 times to counteract that one negative expression.

Remember, your self-talk, how you walk, and your body language are skills. If your scale is tipped heavily to the negative side, you have become very skilled at these negative expressions. Like changing any skill, to get rid of these bad ones, you have to identify better skills, make a commitment to changing them, and practice the positive skills until they're ingrained and automatic.

Thought-stopping. As a well-known psychologist once said, "We become what we think of most of the time." If you're always thinking negatively, then you will likely fail. Another useful technique to reduce your negative thinking and develop your positive thinking is called thought-stopping. This strategy involves replacing your negative self-talk with positive self-talk. Using the Thought Stopping Exercise (see page 55), list the negative statements you commonly say to yourself when you're training and racing. Next, indicate where and in what situations you say the negative things. This will help you become aware of the situations in which you're most likely to be negative. Then, list positive statements with which you can replace them. For example, after a bad race, you might say "I had a horrible race." Instead, replace that negative statement with something more positive such as "I'll work hard and do better in the next time."

The thought-stopping sequence goes as follows. When you start to think or say something negative; say "stop" or "positive," then replace it with a positive statement. As you learn this new skill, you'll become aware of yourself saying negative things before you actually say them and you'll automatically say something positive.

THOUGHT-STOPPING EXERCISE

Directions: In the space below, list common negative thoughts that you have, where and when they occur, and positive statements to place them.

Negative Thoughts	Time, Place Situation	Positive Replacement
1.		
2.		
3.		
4.		
5.		
6.		
7.		
8.		

Ski Racer's Litany. The Ski Racer's Litany is a group of self-statements used to teach positive thinking and increase confidence (see page 57). The litany is like a training drill in which you're focusing on ingraining good technical skills. The litany provides the necessary repetition to instill positive thinking skills.

As I've indicated before, racers are often their own worst enemy. They have a considerable amount of negative thinking and negative self-talk, and this negativity becomes a bad habit. The more racers say negative things, the better they become at being negative. The litany retrains the bad habit of negativity into a good skill of positive thinking. As with any kind of habit, the only way to correct negative thinking is to practice being positive over and over and over again.

A comment I often get from racers when they start using the litany is that they don't believe what they're saying. This is just like the training drill in which racers are making a technical correction. In a sense, their muscles don't "believe" the new skill either. In time, though, the new skill is learned and their muscles come to "believe" it. The same holds true for the positive self-statements. By repeating the litany enough times, racers will start believing it. Just like the improved technique, when they get into a race situation, the new skill of positive thinking will emerge and it will improve their skiing.

The important thing about the Ski Racer's Litany is not only to say it, but to say it like you mean it. For example, I could say "I love to compete, I'm a great ski racer," but I may not sound very convincing. If I say it like I mean it, then I'm more likely to start believing what I'm saying. Saying the litany with conviction also generates positive emotions and physical feelings that will reinforce its positive message.

A great thing about the Ski Racer's Litany is that you can personalize it to your needs. Create your own litany of positive self-statements that means something to you. Then, say the litany out loud every morning and every night. Also, say the litany before you train and race.

SKI RACER'S LITANY

Directions: Repeat the litany when you wake up in the morning, before training and races, before you go to sleep at night, or whenever you have doubts or lose confidence in yourself. Remember to say the litany out loud like you mean it. Also, personalize the litany by adding positive statements that are important to you.

I LOVE TO SKI RACE.

I AM COMMITTED TO BECOMING THE BEST SKI RACER I CAN BE.

I THINK AND TALK POSITIVELY.

I GIVE 100% FOCUS AND INTENSITY WHEN I TRAIN AND RACE.

I AM MY BEST ALLY WHEN I RACE.

IF I FOCUS ON SKIING MY BEST RATHER THAN ON WINNING OR LOSING, I WILL SUCCEED.

I STRIVE TO SKI MY BEST WHEN THE PRESSURE IS ON.

I TRY MY HARDEST REGARDLESS OF THE RESULT.

IF I GIVE MY BEST EFFORT, I AM A WINNER.

Keywords. Another useful way to develop your confidence is to use keywords which remind you to be positive and confident. Make a list of words that make you feel positive and good. Then, write them on your equipment where they're visible during training and races. Also, put keywords in noticeable places where you live such as in your bedroom, on your refrigerator door, or in your locker. When you look at a keyword, say it to yourself. Just like the Ski Racer's Litany, every time you see it, it will sink in further until you truly believe it.

Using negative thinking positively. Even though I very much emphasize being positive at all times, the fact is, racers can't always be positive. They don't always ski as well as they want and there is going to be some negative thinking. This awareness was brought home to me at a U.S. Ski Team training camp I worked at some time ago. During the camp, I was constantly emphasizing being positive and not being negative. One night at dinner, several of the racers came up to me and said that sometimes things do just stink and you can't be positive. I realized that negative thinking is normal when you don't ski well and some negative thinking is healthy. It means you care about skiing poorly and want to ski better. Negative thinking can be motivating as well because it's no fun to ski poorly and lose. I got to thinking about how racers could use negative thinking in a positive way. I came up with an important distinction that will determine whether negative thinking helps or hurts skiing.

There are two types of negative thinking: give-up negative thinking and fire-up negative thinking. Give-up negative thinking involves feelings of loss and despair and helplessness, for example, "It's over. I can't ski well today." Racers dwell on past mistakes and failures. It lowers their motivation and confidence, and it takes their focus away from skiing their best. Their intensity also drops because basically they're surrendering and accepting defeat. There is never a place in ski racing for give-up negative thinking.

In contrast, fire-up negative thinking involves feelings of anger and energy, of being psyched up, for example, "I'm doing so badly. I hate skiing this way" (said with anger and intensity). Racers look to doing better in the future because they hate skiing poorly and losing. Fire-up negative thinking increases their motivation to fight and turn things around. Their intensity goes up and they're bursting with energy. Their focus is on attacking and skiing fast in the next run or race.

Fire-up negative thinking can be a positive way to turn your races around. if you're going to be negative, make sure you use fire-up negative thinking. Don't use it too much though. Negative thinking and negative emotions require a lot of energy and that energy should be put in a more positive direction for your training and races. Also, it doesn't feel very good to be angry all of the time.

> *"Those who win have supreme confidence in their ability, and they are not afraid to take chances."*
>
> **Zach Crist**

CONFIDENCE CHALLENGE

The real test of confidence is how you respond when things are not going your way. I call this the Confidence Challenge. It's easy to stay confident when you're skiing well, when the conditions are ideal, and when you're competing against a weak field. But as I said earlier, an inevitable part of ski racing is that you'll have some down periods. What separates the best from the rest is that the best racers are able to maintain their confidence when they're not skiing their best. By staying confident, they continue to work hard rather than give up because they know that, in time, their skiing will come around.

Most racers when they ski poorly lose their confidence and get caught in the vicious cycle of low confidence and poor performance. Once they slip into that downward spiral, they rarely can get out of it. In contrast, racers with prime confidence maintain their confidence and seek out ways to return to their previous level. All racers will go through periods where they don't ski well. The skill is not getting caught in the vicious cycle and being able to get out of the down periods quickly.

The Confidence Challenge can be thought of as a Prime Ski Racing skill that can be developed. Learning to respond positively to the Confidence Challenge comes from exposing yourself to demanding situations, difficult conditions, and tough competition in training and races and practicing positive responses.

There are several key aspects of mastering the Confidence Challenge. First, you need to develop the attitude that demanding situations are challenges to be sought out rather than threats to be avoided. When you're faced with a Confidence Challenge you must see it as an opportunity to become a better ski racer. You also need to believe that experiencing challenges is a necessary part of becoming the best ski racer you can be. You have to realize that, at first, these challenges are going to be uncomfortable because they are difficult and unfamiliar. As you expose yourself to more challenges, they will become less threatening and more comfortable.

With this perspective, you should seek out every possible challenge in training and races. Be sure you're well-prepared to meet the challenges. You can't master the Confidence Challenge if you don't have the preparation and skills to do so. Stay positive and motivated in the face of the difficulties. Don't allow yourself to be sucked into the vicious cycle. Then, focus on what you need to do to overcome the challenge rather than on how difficult it may be or how you may fail. Also, accept that you'll make mistakes and may not fully succeed when faced with a challenge for the first time. Don't take this as a failure, but rather as an experience you can learn from to improve next time. Finally, and most importantly, never, ever give up!

"You tell your mind what to do and if you're able to fuel your mind with positive thoughts and confidence, you'll achieve amazing things."

1984 Olympic marathon champion Joan Benoit-Samuelson

CHAPTER FOUR:

INTENSITY

PRIME SKI RACING

Intensity

Confidence

Motivation

Intensity may be the most important contributor to performance just before the race. It's so important because all of the motivation, confidence, focus, and emotions in the world won't help you if your body is not physiologically capable of doing what it needs to do in order for you to ski your best.

Simply put, intensity is the amount of physiological activity you experience in your body including heart rate, respiration, and adrenaline. Intensity is a continuum that ranges from sleep (very relaxed) to terror (very anxious). Somewhere in between those two extremes is the level of intensity at which you ski your best.

Intensity is made up of two components. First, there is the physical experience of intensity, that is, what you actually feel in your body when you are in the start area before a race. Are you calm or filled with energy? Are you relaxed or tense? Second, there is your perception of the intensity. In other words, do you perceive the intensity positively or negatively? Two racers can feel the exact same thing physiologically, but interpret those physical feelings in very different ways. One may view the intensity as excitement and it will help his skiing. Another may see the intensity as anxiety and it will hurt his skiing.

The physical experience and the perception of intensity are affected by several mental factors. If you are not confident, feeling frustrated and angry, and focusing on winning rather than on skiing your best, you will see the intensity as negative. In contrast, if you are confident and positive, happy and excited, and focused on skiing well, the intensity will be perceived as positive.

Signs of Over-and Under-intensity

Intensity produces a wide variety of physical and mental symptoms that can help you recognize when your intensity is too high or too low. By being aware of these signs, you will be able to know when you're not skiing at prime intensity and can take steps to reach that ideal level.

Overintensity. Muscle tension and breathing difficulties are the most common signs of overintensity. Most racers indicate that when they're too intense, they feel tension in their shoulders and their legs, which happen to be the two most important physical areas for ski racing. For example, if a racer's legs are tense, he loses the ability to ski with power, agility, and suppleness.

Many racers also report that their breathing becomes short and choppy when they get nervous. This restriction in breathing means that they're not getting enough oxygen into their system so they will tire quickly. I've also found that the smoothness of racers' movement tends to mirror their breathing. If their breathing is long and smooth, so is their movement. If their breathing is abrupt and choppy, their movement is jerky and uncomfortable.

Racers who are overly intense often exhibit poor posture. Muscle tension causes their shoulders to rise and their body to seem to close up. Racers make more mistakes when they're overly intense because anxiety disrupts coordination. Overintensity interferes with motor control that affects technical skills and movement. Racers often look rushed and frantic in the start area.

Overintensity negatively influences racers mentally as well. Anxiety lowers confidence and causes doubts in ability. The physical and mental discomfort produces negative emotions such as frustration, anger, and depression. The anxiety, doubts, and negative emotions hurt focus by drawing racers' attention away from skiing their best and onto how badly they feel.

Underintensity. Though not as common, racers can also experience underintensity before races. The most common symptom of underintensity is low energy and lethargy. Racers lack the adrenaline they need to give their best effort. Though not as discomforting as overintensity, underintensity hurts skiing equally because racers lack the physical requisites such as strength, stamina, and agility to meet the demands of a race.

Mentally, underintensity undermines motivation. Racers just don't feel like being out there. The lack of interest caused by too low intensity also impairs their focus because they're easily distracted and have difficulty staying focused on their skiing.

> *"My hands get sweaty, I lose my balance, and my legs feel hollow."*
>
> **Casey Puckett**

LINE BETWEEN INTENSITY AND TENSITY

The ultimate goal of prime intensity is to find the precise line between intensity and tensity. The closer racers can get to that line, the more their body will work for them in achieving Prime Ski Racing. If racers cross the line to tensity, their body will no longer be physically capable of attaining Prime Ski Racing. Great racers have the ability to do two things related to this line. First, they have a better understanding of where that line is, so they can "tightrope walk" on it, thereby maximizing what their body can give them. Second, they're able to stay on that line longer than other racers, which enables them to ski at a consistently higher level for longer periods of time.

"Pressure is only as big as you let it be."

Benjamin Raich

PRIME INTENSITY

Prime intensity is the ideal amount of physiological activity necessary for racers to ski their best. It is also the level of intensity that racers perceive as most positive and beneficial to their skiing. Unfortunately, there is no one ideal level of intensity for every racer. Prime intensity is individual; it's different for everyone. Some racers ski best relaxed. Others ski best energized, but not too psyched up. Still others ski best unbelievably intense and fired up. Racers must find out the level of intensity that enables them to ski their best.

You have several goals in developing prime intensity. First, to learn what is your prime intensity. Then, to recognize the signs of overintensity and underintensity. Next, to identify competitive situations in which your intensity may go up or down. Finally, to take active steps to reach and maintain prime intensity throughout a race day.

Your intensity is much like the thermostat maintaining the most comfortable temperature in your house. You always notice when your house is too warm or too cold because you're sensitive to changes in temperature. When the temperature becomes uncomfortable, you adjust the thermostat to a more comfortable level. You can think of your intensity as your internal temperature that needs to be adjusted periodically. You need to be sensitive to when your intensity is no longer comfortable, in other words, it's not allowing you to ski your best. You can then use the intensity control techniques I'll be describing to you to raise or lower your intensity to its prime level.

DETERMINING PRIME INTENSITY

Using the Intensity Identification form (see page 67), you can identify what is your prime intensity. First, think back to several races in which you skied very well. Recall your level of intensity. Were you relaxed, energized, or really fired up? Then remember the thoughts, emotions, and physical feelings you experienced during these races. Were you positive or negative, happy or angry, relaxed or tense? Second, think back to several races in which you skied poorly. Recall your level of intensity. Remember the thoughts, emotions, and physical feelings you had in these races. If you're like most racers, a distinct pattern will emerge. When you ski well, you have a particular level of intensity. This is your prime intensity. There are also common thoughts, emotions, and physical feelings associated with skiing well. In contrast, when you're skiing poorly, there is a very different level of intensity, either higher or lower than your prime intensity. There are also decidedly different thoughts, emotions, and physical feelings.

Another useful way to help you understand your prime intensity is to experiment with different levels of intensity in training and see how the differing intensity impacts your skiing. Here is a good exercise you can use to learn more about your prime intensity:

Let's say you're going to take six training runs of slalom. Break up the training session into three segments. The first segment will emphasize low intensity. Before you begin the run, take several slow, deep breaths, relax your muscles, and focus on calming thoughts (e.g., "Easy does it," "Cool and calm."). As you start the run, stay focused on keeping your body relaxed and calm.

The second segment will focus on moderate intensity. Before the run, take a few deep, but stronger breaths, jump around a bit, and focus on more energetic thoughts (e.g., "Let's go," "Pick it up."). Before the run, bounce on your skis lightly and feel your intensity picking up. During the run, pay attention to feeling the intensity and energy in your body.

The final segment will highlight high intensity. Before the run, take several deep, forced breaths with special emphasis on a hard and aggressive exhale, start bouncing up and down on your skis immediately, and repeat intense thoughts (e.g., "Fire it up," "Get after it."), saying these out loud with energy and force. Feel the high level of intensity and energy as you begin the run, and focus on maintaining the intensity throughout the turn.

I encourage you to use this exercise for several days so you can see clearly how your intensity impacts your skiing. As with the Intensity Identification form, you will probably see a pattern emerge in which you ski better at one of the three levels of intensity. With this knowledge, you will have a good sense of your prime intensity and can then use that information to recognize when you're not at prime intensity and when you need to adjust your intensity to a prime level.

I should also point out that prime intensity may differ between events. The feedback I get from many racers is that the technical events usually require a higher level of intensity than the speed events. However, this view in not unanimous. You should use the Intensity Identification form and the training experiment that I just described to determine your prime intensity for each event.

"Every day I trained at 100 percent World Cup intensity. You have to eat, breath, sleep, and live that intensity."

USST member Chad Fleischer

INTENSITY IDENTIFICATION

Directions: In the space below, indicate the mental and physical factors that are related to your best (prime intensity) and worst (overintensity or underintensity) races. At the bottom, summarize the positive and negative factors that distinguish your prime from poor intensity.

	Best Races	Worst Races
Importance of race		
Difficulty of competition		
Race conditions		
Thoughts		
Emotions		
Physical feelings		

PSYCH-DOWN TECHNIQUES

When you're in a big race, it's natural for your intensity to go up and for you to feel nervous. If you want to ski your best, you have to take active steps to get your intensity back to its prime level. There are several simple techniques you can use to help you get your intensity back under control.

Deep breathing. When racers experience overintensity, one of the first things that's disrupted is their breathing. It becomes short and choppy and they don't get the oxygen their body needs to ski its best. The most basic way to lower their intensity then is to take control of their breathing again by focusing on taking slow, deep breaths.

Deep breathing has several important benefits. It ensures that you get enough oxygen so your body can function well. By getting more oxygen into your body, you will relax, feel better, and it will give you a greater sense of control. This increased comfort will give you more confidence and enable you to more easily combat negative thoughts. It will also help you let go of negative emotions such as frustration and anger, and allow you to regain positive emotions such as excitement. Focusing on your breathing also acts to take your mind off of things that may be interfering with your racing and back onto things that will enable you to ski better.

Deep breathing should be a part of your between-run routine (to be discussed further in Chapter Eight). One place in particular where deep breathing can be especially valuable to reduce intensity is before you begin a training or race run. If you take two deep breaths at this point, you ensure that your body is relaxed and comfortable, and you're focused on something that will help you ski your best.

Muscle relaxation. The most common sign of overintensity is muscle tension. This is the most crippling physical symptom because if your muscles are tight and stiff, you won't be able to ski at your highest level. There are two muscle relaxation techniques, passive relaxation and active relaxation, you can use off the hill or, in a shortened form, before training or race runs. Similar to deep breathing, muscle relaxation is beneficial because it allows you to regain control of your body and to make you feel more comfortable physically. It also offers the same mental and emotional advantages as does deep breathing.

Passive relaxation involves imagining that tension is a liquid that fills your muscles creating discomfort that interferes with your body performing its best. By imagining that you have drain plugs on the bottom of your feet, the tension can drain out of your body and you can attain a desired state of relaxation.

To prepare for passive relaxation, lie down in a comfortable position in a quiet place where you won't be disturbed. Use the passive relaxation procedure described on page 71. You can memorize the procedure, have someone guide you through it, or record it on an audiotape and listen to it on your own. As you go through the passive relaxation procedure, take your time, focus on your breathing and your muscles, feel the tension leave your body, and, at the end, focus on your overall state of mental calmness and physical relaxation.

Active relaxation is used when your body is very tense and you can't relax your muscles with passive relaxation. When your intensity is too high and your muscles are tight, it's difficult to just relax them. So instead of trying to relax your muscles, do just the opposite. Tighten them more, then release them. Our muscles work on what is called an opponent principle process. For example, before a race, your muscle tension might be at an 8, where 1 is totally relaxed and 10 is very tense, but you ski best at a 4. By further tightening your muscles up to a 10 , the natural reaction is for your muscles to rebound back past 8 toward a more relaxed 4. So, making your muscles more tense actually causes them to become more relaxed.

Active relaxation typically involves tightening and relaxing four major muscle groups: face and neck, arms and shoulders, chest and back, and buttocks and legs. It can also be individualized to focus on particular muscles that trouble you the most.

To get ready for active relaxation follow the same preparations as I described for passive relaxation, Use the active relaxation procedure described on page 72. The most important part of active relaxation is learning to tell the difference between states of tension and relaxation. As you go through the active relaxation procedure, focus on the differences between tension and relaxation, be aware of how you are able to induce a greater feeling of relaxation, and, at the end, focus on your overall state of mental calmness and physical relaxation.

These two relaxation procedures can also be used between runs in an abbreviated form. Just before your training or race run, you can allow the tension to drain out of tense parts of your body using passive relaxation or you can do a set of active relaxation on tense muscles.

PASSIVE RELAXATION

Imagine there are drain plugs on the bottom of your feet. When you open them, all the tension will drain out of your body and you will become very, very relaxed. Take a slow, deep breath.

Now, undo those plugs. Feel the tension begin to drain out of your body. Down from the top of your head, past your forehead, your face and neck; you're becoming more and more relaxed. The tension drains out of your jaw and down past your neck. Now your face and your neck are warm and relaxed and comfortable. Take a slow, deep breath.

The tension continues to drain out of your upper body, past your hands and forearms, and out of your upper arms and shoulders. Now your hands, arms and shoulders are warm and relaxed and comfortable. Take a slow, deep breath.

The tension continues to drain out of your upper body, past your chest and upper back, down past your stomach and lower back, and your upper body is becoming more and more relaxed. There is no more tension left in your upper body. Now your entire upper body is warm and relaxed and comfortable. Take a slow, deep breath.

The tension continues to drain out of your lower body, past your buttocks and down past your thighs and your knees. Your lower body is becoming more and more relaxed. The tension drains out of your calves. There is almost no more tension left in your body and the last bit of tension drains past your ankles, the balls of your feet, and your toes. Now do a brief survey of your body from head to toe to ensure that there is no more tension left in your body. Your entire body is warm and relaxed and comfortable. Now replace the plugs so that no tension can get back in. Take a slow, deep breath. Feel the calm and relaxation envelop you. Enjoy that feeling and remember what it feels like to be completely relaxed.

ACTIVE RELAXATION

When I say tight, I want you to tighten that body part for five seconds; when I say loose, I want you to relax it.

First, your buttocks and legs. Tight...loose. Feel the relaxation. Take a slow, deep breath. Once again with the buttocks and legs. Tight...loose. The muscles in your buttocks and legs are warm and relaxed. Feel the difference between the states of tension and relaxation in your buttocks and legs. Take a slow, deep breath.

Now your chest and back. Tight...loose. Feel the relaxation. Take a slow, deep breath. Once again with the chest and back. Tight...loose. The muscles in your chest and back are warm and relaxed. Feel the difference between the states of tension and relaxation in your chest and back. Take a slow, deep breath.

Now your arms and shoulders. Tight...loose. Feel the relaxation. Take a slow, deep breath. Once again with the arms and shoulders. Tight...loose. The muscles in your arms and shoulders are warm and relaxed. Feel the difference between the states of tension and relaxation in your arms and shoulders. Take a slow, deep breath.

Now your face and neck. Tight...loose. Feel the relaxation. Take a slow, deep breath. Once again with the face and neck. Tight...loose. The muscles in your face and neck are warm and relaxed. Feel the difference between the states of tension and relaxation in your face and neck. Take a slow, deep breath.

Now every muscle in your body. Be sure that every muscle is as tight as you can get it. Tight...loose. Feel the relaxation. Take a slow, deep breath. Once again with your entire body. Tight...loose. Every muscle in your body is warm and relaxed. Feel the difference between the states of tension and relaxation in your entire body. Take a slow, deep breath.

Now do a mental check list to make sure that every muscle is relaxed. Your feet are relaxed, calves, thighs, buttocks, stomach, back, chest, arms, shoulders, neck, and face. Every muscle in your body is completely relaxed.

Slow pace of pre-race preparation. A common side effect of overintensity is that racers tend to speed up the pace of their pre-race preparation. Racers can rush around the start area as if they want to get the race over with as soon as possible. So, to lower your intensity, slow your pace as you go through your pre-race routine. Simply slowing your pace and giving yourself time to slow your breathing and relax your muscles will help you lower your intensity to its prime level.

Process focus. One of the primary causes of overintensity is focusing on the outcome of the race. If you're worried about whether you will win or lose, you're bound to get nervous. The prospect of losing is threatening, so that will make you anxious. The thought of winning, especially if it's against a tough field, can also be anxiety provoking because it may be unfamiliar or unexpected to you.

To reduce the anxiety caused by an outcome focus, redirect your focus onto the process. Ask yourself, what do I need to do to ski my best? This process focus can include paying attention to your technique or tactics. Or it might involve focusing on mental skills such as positive thinking or the psych-down strategies I am currently describing. You can also shift your focus onto your breathing which will take your mind off of the outcome and will directly relax your body by providing more oxygen to your system.

A process focus takes your mind off things that cause your over-intensity and shifts your focus onto things that will reduce your anxiety, build your confidence, and give you a greater sense of control over your skiing (to be discussed further in Chapter Five).

Keywords. Another focusing technique for lowering your intensity is to use what I call intensity keywords. These words act as reminders of what you need to do with your intensity to ski your best (see Intensity Keywords on page 75). Keywords are especially important just before a race run when you can get so wrapped up in the pressure that you forget to do the things you need to do in order to ski your best. By saying the keyword before a race run, you'll be reminded to use the psych-down techniques when your intensity starts to go up. I also recommend that you write one or two key-words on a piece of tape which you then put on your gloves or skis. Looking at the keywords acts as a further reminder to follow the keywords and lower your intensity.

INTENSITY KEYWORDS

Directions: A variety of intensity keywords have been provided below. In the space at the bottom, identify other intensity keywords that you can use.

Psych-Down	Psych-Up
Breathe	Go For It
Loose	Charge
Relax	Attack
Calm	Positive
Easy	Hustle
Trust	Commit

Music. Music is one of the most common tools racers use to control their intensity before races. We all know that music has a profound physical and emotional impact on us. Music has the ability to make us happy, sad, inspired, and motivated. Music can also excite or relax us. Many World Cup racers can be seen listening to music during inspection, on their warm-up runs, and in the start area before their race runs to help them reach their prime intensity.

Music is beneficial in several ways. It has a direct effect on you physically. Calming music slows your breathing and relaxes your muscles. Simply put, it makes you feel good. Mentally, it makes you feel positive and motivated. It also generates positive emotions such as joy and contentment. Finally, calming music takes your mind off aspects of the race that may cause doubt or anxiety. The overall sensation of listening to relaxing music is a generalized sense of peace and well-being.

Smile. The last technique for lowering intensity is one of the strangest and most effective I've ever come across. A few years ago, I was working with a USST racer who was having a terrible training session. She was skiing poorly and her coach was getting frustrated with her. She approached me before a training run feeling angry and depressed, and her body was in knots. She asked me what she could do. I didn't have a good answer until an idea just popped into my head. I told her to smile. She said, I don't want to smile. I told her to smile. She said she was not happy and didn't want to smile. I told her again to smile. This time, just to get me off her back, she did smile. I told her to hold the smile. During the next two minutes there was an amazing transformation. As she stood there with the smile on her face, the tension began to drain out of her body. Her breathing became slow and deep. She said that she was feeling better. In a short time, she was looking more relaxed and happier. She returned to training, her skiing improved immediately, and she made some progress during the remainder of the training session.

Her response was so dramatic that I wanted to learn how such a change could occur. When I returned to my office, I looked at the research related to smiling and learned two things. First, as we grow up, we become conditioned to the positive effects of smiling. In other words, we learn that when we smile, it means we're happy and life is good. Second, there's been some fascinating research looking at the effects of smiling on our brain chemistry. What this research has found is that when we smile, it releases brain chemicals called endorphines which have an actual physiologically relaxing effect.

> *"Deep breathing and other relaxation techniques and visualization are the way most racers spend the minute prior to the race. Eddie Podivinsky jumps around and Matt Grosjean builds inner energy and focus."*
>
> ### *Ski Racing* Survey

PSYCH-UP TECHNIQUES

Though less common, letdowns in intensity can also cause your level of skiing to decline. A decrease in intensity causes all the things that enable you to ski well to disappear. Physically, you no longer have the blood flow, oxygen, and adrenaline necessary for the strength, agility, and stamina you need to ski your best. Mentally, you lose the motivation and focus that enables you to ski well. Just like psych-down techniques when your intensity is too high, you can use psych-up techniques to raise your intensity when it drops.

Intense breathing. Just as deep breathing can reduce intensity, intense breathing can increase it. If you find your intensity dropping, several hard exhales can take your body and your mind to a more intense level. A useful technique to use before a training or race run is to take two intense breaths. In fact, I encourage you to make intense breathing a part of your training and pre-race routines when you're intensity goes down (to be discussed further in Chapter Eight).

Move your body. Remember that intensity is, most basically, physiological activity. The most direct way to increase intensity is with physical action. In other words, move. Walk or run around, jump up and down. Anything to get your heart pumping and your body going.

High-energy self-talk. One of the main causes of drops in intensity is let-down thoughts. Thinking to yourself, "I've got this won" or "I can't win this," will result in your intensity decreasing. When this happens, you can be sure your skiing will decline. When you start to have these thoughts, you need to replace them with high-energy self-talk. Self-talk such as "Keep attacking" and "Go for it" will keep you motivated and focused, and your body will respond with more intensity.

Intensity keywords. Just as you can use keywords to lower intensity, they can also be used to counter letdowns and to psych yourself up (see Intensity Keywords on page 75). Saying intensity keywords such as "Charge" and "Hustle" with conviction and energy will raise your intensity and generate positive thoughts and emotions that will enable you to ski your best.

High-energy body language. It's difficult using high-energy self-talk and intensity keywords without also having high-energy body language. Pumping your fist or slapping your thigh will also get you fired up and will increase your intensity.

Music. The value of music has already been described above. Music can also be used to raise your intensity and get you psyched up and motivated. The overall sensation of listening to high-energy music is a generalized sense of excitement and energy.

> *"I have a set of key words that I always say at the same time in the gate to create the same frame of mind when I'm on course. When the 10-second buzzer goes I say, 'The snow leopard attacks, he attacks, he attacks, he always attacks.' That takes me to six seconds, and I say, 'Let's go, let's get after this thing, let's see how much speed you can get out of this thing.' Then I kick out of the gate."*
>
> **Chad Fleischer**

CHAPTER FIVE:

FOCUS

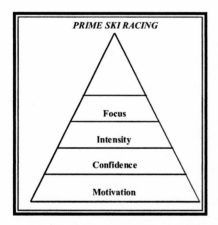

Focus is the most misunderstood mental factor among racers. Most racers think of focus as concentrating on one thing for a long time. They see it as intense and effortful. But ski racing is not like that. There are many different things that racers must focus on before and during a race.

Let me introduce a term, attentional field, and then I'll define focus for you. Attentional field is everything inside of you, such as thoughts, emotions, and physical responses, and everything outside of you, including sights and sounds, on which you could focus. Focus is the ability to attend to internal and external cues in your attentional field.

Prime focus involves focusing only on performance-relevant cues in your attentional field. In other words, only focusing on cues that help you ski your best. Performance-relevant cues can include the course, snow conditions, technique, and the terrain. Prime focus gives you the ability to adjust your focus internally before a race and externally while you are on course.

For example, a racer directs her focus externally while inspecting. She then focuses internally during her pre-race preparation in the start area during which time she uses mental imagery and checks her intensity. When she gets in the starting gate, she turns her focus outward again onto the course.

Poor focus involves focusing on performance-irrelevant cues in your attentional field. That is, focusing on cues that will hurt your skiing. There are two types of harmful cues. Interfering cues are those that will directly hurt your skiing such as negative thoughts, anxiety, and concern over results. Irrelevant cues are those that simply distract you from an effective focus including what you'll have for dinner tonight or the project that you must finish by tomorrow.

> *"Any thoughts about something going on at another time destroy your focus. You can't be thinking about the results; you have to be thinking about what you're doing right now."*
>
> **Casey Puckett**

FOCUS STYLES

One of the most important developments I've made in my work in recent years is in understanding the importance of identifying racers' focus styles. A focus style is a preference for paying attention to certain cues. Racers tend to be more comfortable focusing on some cues and avoid or don't pay attention to other cues. Every racer has a dominant style that impacts all aspects of their skiing. This dominant style will surface most noticeably when they're under pressure. The two types of focus styles are internal and external.

Internal focus style. Racers with an internal focus style ski best when they're totally and consistently focused on their skiing during training or a race. They need to keep their focus narrow, thinking only about their skiing. These racers tend to be easily distracted by activity in their immediate surroundings. If they broaden their focus and take their mind off their skiing, for example, if they talk about non-skiing topics with their friends before a race, they'll become distracted and will have trouble narrowing their focus back onto their skiing.

External focus style. Racers with an external focus style ski best when they only focus on their skiing when they're about to begin a training or race run. At all other times, they broaden their focus and take their mind off their skiing. These racers have a tendency to think too much and become negative and critical. This overly narrow focus causes them to lose confidence and experience overintensity. For these racers, it's essential that they take their focus away from their skiing when they're not training or racing.

External focus style runs counter to beliefs held by many coaches. They think that if racers are not totally focused on their skiing, then they're not serious about it and they won't ski their best. Yet, for racers with an external focus style, they don't want to think too much or be too serious because this causes them to be negative and critical. They'll ski their best when they're not thinking too much about their skiing and they simply allow their natural abilities to emerge on their own.

> *I am aware of what's going on around me, but I'm not paying attention, because I don't care what anyone else is doing."*
>
> **Olympic champion Picabo Street**

IDENTIFYING YOUR FOCUS STYLE

With this understanding, you need to identify what is your focus style. Are you a racer who needs to keep your mind on your skiing constantly in order for you to ski well? Or are you someone who thinks too much and needs to keep your mind off your skiing until its time to perform?

Recall past races when you've skied well. Were you totally focused on your skiing before the race or were you keeping your mind off your skiing? Also, recall past races when you've skied poorly. Were you thinking too much or were you distracted by things going on around you? If you're like most racers, a pattern will emerge in which you tend to ski best when you focus one way and you ski poorly when you focus another way.

Understanding your focus style is essential for you to be able to manage it effectively. This process involves knowing how you focus best and actively focusing in a way that is consistent with your focus style. This ability to manage your focus style well is most essential in important races. There is a tendency for racers under pressure to revert back to a focus style that will interfere rather than help their skiing. For example, if you're someone who skis best with an external focus style, you may find yourself turning your focus inward when the pressure is on. You may start to think too much and become negative and critical.

When you start to lose your prime focus style under pressure, you must become aware that you're moving away from it and that you need to take steps to redirect your focus back to the style that works best for you. Continuing the previous example, when you realize that you're focusing internally too much, you should actively turn your focus outward by looking around and taking your mind off your skiing.

Mag-Lite® Focus

I've developed a useful tool to help you understand your focus style and to develop focus control. A Mag-Lite® is a flashlight whose beam can be adjusted to illuminate a wide area or to brighten a narrow area. Your focus can be thought of as a Mag-Lite® beam you project that illuminates on what you want to focus.

Racers with an internal focus style want to keep their Mag-Lite® beam narrow at all times, only illuminating skiing-related things during training or races. If you have an internal focus style, your goal is to stay focused on necessary training or race cues and to block out unnecessary external distractions. To accomplish this, narrow your Mag-Lite® beam by keeping your eyes within the confines of the training or race setting and avoid talking to others. Focus on important skiing cues, for example, line, snow conditions, or intensity.

Racers with an external focus style want to widen their Mag-Lite® beam before training and race runs to take their mind off their skiing, then narrow their beam shortly before the next run. If you have an external focus style, your goal is to direct your focus off your skiing before runs. To do this, when you're not actually skiing, whether in training or a race, widen your Mag-Lite® beam by looking around you and talking to your coach or other racers. This will keep you from thinking too much and becoming negative and critical. Shortly before you begin your next run, narrow your Mag-Lite® beam, focusing specifically on something that will help you ski well.

There are also times when, regardless of your focus styles, you'll need to narrow or widen your Mag-Lite® beam. For example, you will want to broaden your Mag-Lite® beam when you're receiving course information from your coach or you're watching racers go before you. You will want to narrow your Mag-Lite® beam to check your intensity and to review the course using race imagery in the start area.

> *"The starter gave me the "Racer ready...go!" I put my poles over the wand and my world went silent."*
>
> **USST member Kristina Koznick**

FOCUS CONTROL

Developing focus control is essential if you're going to ensure that your focus style helps rather than hurts your skiing. There are several steps in the focus control process. First, you have to identify your focus style and understand how it impacts your skiing. Next, you must recognize internal and external cues that help and hurt your skiing. Finally, you have to adjust your focus internally and externally as needed during training and races.

The eyes have it. We obtain most of our information about the world through our eyes. The most direct way to control our Mag-Lite® beam is to control our eyes. You can think of your eyes as Mag-Lite® flashlights that you can adjust wide or narrow. If you want to minimize the external distractions during training or races, narrow your Mag-Lite® beam by keeping your eyes down and on the course. If you're distracted by something, either look away or turn away from it. If you're not looking at something, it can't distract you.

Conversely, if you find that you're thinking too much or being negative or critical, widen your Mag-Lite® beam by raising your eyes and looking around you. For example, watch the skier before you or talk to other racers around you. By looking around, you'll be distracted from your thoughts, you'll be able to clear your mind, and then you can narrow your Mag-Lite® beam in preparation for your run.

Outcome vs. process focus. Perhaps the greatest obstacle to prime focus is having an outcome focus before a race. Outcome focus involves focusing on the possible results of a race: winning, losing, rankings, or who you might defeat or lose to. I tell racers that an outcome focus is the kiss of death in ski racing.

Many racers believe that by focusing on the outcome, that is, on winning the race, they're more likely to achieve that outcome. What most racers don't realize is that having an outcome focus actually hurts performance and makes it less likely that they will win. Every time racers shift from a process focus to an outcome focus, their skiing will decline. This drop in performance occurs for several reasons. First, racers are no longer focusing on things that will help them ski well. Second, it causes their intensity to move away from prime intensity, either up because they start to get nervous over the possibility of losing, or down because racers think they already have the race won.

Racers don't understand several key things about outcome focus. The outcome comes after the process has occurred and the race is over. The outcome is totally unrelated to the process of the race. In fact, the result of an outcome focus is usually the exact opposite of the outcome racers want—to achieve Prime Ski Racing and have a successful race.

The way to achieve the desired outcome of the race is to focus on the process of the race. Process focus involves focusing on aspects of the race that will enable you to ski your best, for example, technique, tactics, intensity, or emotions. If you ski your best, you're more likely to have a successful race.

Focus on what you can control. A major focusing problem I see with many racers is that they focus on things over which they have no control. Racers worry about their competition, the weather, or the conditions, to name a few things outside of racers' control. This focus has no value because they can't do anything about those things. This kind of focus hurts performance because it lowers confidence and causes worry and anxiety. It also distracts racers from what they need to focus on. The fact is, there's only one thing that racers can control, and that is themselves. For example, their attitude, thoughts, emotions, and intensity. If racers focus on those things, they'll be more confident and relaxed, and they'll be better able to focus on what they need to do in order to ski their best.

Four P's. I have a general rule you can follow that will help you identify what kinds of things you should focus on in your skiing. I call it the four P's. The first P is *positive*. You should focus on positive things that will help your skiing and avoid negative things that will hurt it. The second P is *process*. As I've just explained, you should focus on what you need to do to ski your best. The third P is *present*. You should focus on what you need to do right now to ski well at this moment. You shouldn't focus on the past because it's out of your control and you can't change it. You also shouldn't focus on the future because it's too far away to do anything about. The only way to control the future is to control the present. The only way to control the present is to focus on it. The last P is *progress*. There's a tendency for many racers to compare themselves with other racers, seeing others having better results and getting ahead of them in the rankings. How your competition skis is outside of your control. What you should focus on is your improvement. Racers develop at different rates. A racer who is ahead of you now may not even be in sight behind you in a year. What's important is that you see yourself progressing toward the goals you want to achieve.

> *"If I find myself thinking about how the results will go, I have to try and correct myself and think about something else."*
>
> **World champion Hilary Lindh**

FOCUSING VS. THINKING

A mistake many racers make is that they equate focusing with thinking. They believe that if they're thinking about, for example, an upcoming race run, then they're also focusing on it and it will help their skiing. However, there is a big difference between racers focusing on their skiing and thinking about their skiing. This distinction impacts not only racers' ability to concentrate on important aspects of their skiing, but it also affects their motivation, confidence, intensity, and emotions.

Focusing simply involves attending to internal or external cues. This process is impartial, objective, unemotional, and detached from judgment or evaluation. If you make a mistake on something on which you were focusing, you're able to accept it and not be overly disappointed by the failure. In a focusing mode, you're able to use the failure as information to correct the problem and focus better in the future.

In contrast, thinking is connected to your ego-investment in your skiing, that is, how important your skiing is to you. Thinking is judgmental and critical. If you make a mistake or ski poorly when you're in a thinking mode, it hurts your confidence and causes negative emotions such as frustration and anger. Thinking actually interferes with your ability to focus in a way that will help your skiing and it will cause your skiing to deteriorate.

> *"You can't think and hit at the same time."*
>
> **Baseball legend Yogi Berra**

Chapter Six:

Emotions

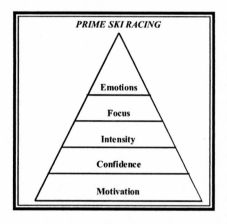

At the top of the Prime Ski Racing Pyramid sits emotions. It is closest to the top of the pyramid because emotions will ultimately dictate how you ski in races. Emotions before, during, and after a race can cover the spectrum from excitement and joy to frustration and anger. Emotions are often strong and, most troublesome, they can linger and hurt skiing long after you first experience them.

Negative emotions hurt skiing both physically and mentally. They first cause racers to lose their prime intensity. With frustration and anger, intensity goes up and leads to muscle tension, breathing difficulties, and a loss of coordination. It also saps energy and causes racers to tire quickly. When racers experience despair and helplessness, their intensity drops sharply and they no longer have the physical capabilities to ski well.

Negative emotions also hurt racers mentally. Fundamentally, negative emotions are a response to the perceived threat that racers will fail. Their emotions are telling them that, deep down, they're not confident in their ability to ski well and to have a successful race. Their confidence will decline and they will have more negative thoughts to go along with their negative emotions. Also, since negative emotions are so strong, racers will have difficulty focusing on what will help them to ski well. The negative emotions draw their attention onto all of the negative aspects of their skiing. Finally, negative emotions hurt racers' motivation to ski because it's no longer fun and they just don't feel good.

Emotions come from past experiences in similar situations in the form of beliefs and attitudes racers hold about skiing and competing. The emotions associated with these beliefs and attitudes are commonly known as the "baggage" people carry from their past. Their perceptions from the past impact their present even though the emotions may not be appropriate or useful in the present situation. One of the most difficult aspects of emotions is that they become habits that cause people to automatically respond with a certain emotional reaction to a particular circumstance even when that emotional response does more harm than good.

Negative emotions can be provoked by many occurrences during a race including difficulty memorizing a course, making a mistake during an otherwise strong run, and just skiing poorly. All of these events share two common elements that lie at the heart of what causes the negative emotions: Racers feel that the path to a goal is being blocked and they don't seem to have control over removing the obstacle. For example, a racer is having a poor run and no matter what he tries, he can't seem to turn the run around. The racer is likely to experience frustration and anger initially. These emotions can be helpful at first because they motivate him to fight to clear the path to his goal and regain control of the race. If he's unable to change the course of the race, then he may experience despair and helplessness, in which he accepts that he can not win, so he just gives up.

LET THE PUNISHMENT FIT THE CRIME

In my work with high-level racers, I have seen extremely negative emotional reactions to the smallest failures. A slip in line, a hooked tip in training, produced frustration and anger that seemed to be out of proportion to the magnitude of the failure. For example, a young racer I worked with would beat herself up emotionally for making a mistake in training. Her level of training performance would steadily decline and she would feel terrible about her skiing and herself. By the end of training, she would be battered and bruised by her own emotions. Clearly, the punishment did not fit the crime.

Be sure that your emotions are proportional to what causes them. Ask yourself whether a few mistakes are worth the frustration and anger you might feel and express to yourself. Are you being fair to yourself? When the severity of the punishment exceeds the seriousness of the crime, you have lost perspective on how important your skiing is in your life. It might be worth getting frustrated and angry if you didn't get into the college of your choice or you lost your job, but are these strong negative emotions worth feeling over some unimportant mistakes?

You should also consider whether these emotions help or hurt your skiing. Negative emotions can raise your skiing at first because they increase your intensity and get you to fight harder. After a short time though, your skiing begins to decline and it usually spirals downward into a vicious cycle from there. Negative emotions actually hurt your skiing and keep you from reaching your goals. Why would you allow yourself to experience emotions (frustration, anger, depression) and act in a way (throwing a tantrum, choking, giving up) that ensures failure rather than helps you achieve success?

It's okay to be disappointed when you make mistakes or lose. In fact, you should feel that way. It means that you care about your skiing and want to do better. But when your emotions are stronger and more hurtful than they should be given how minor the crime is and how often it occurs (you will make a lot of mistakes during your skiing career), then you need to look at why your punishment far exceeds the crime you committed.

Look at the best racers in the world. Ski racing is very important to them because it is their life and livelihood. How upset do they get when they ski poorly and lose? Some get very upset. Overall, though, considering how important ski racing is to them, most great racers handle mistakes and losses pretty well. In fact, one reason why the best racers in the world are at the top is because they have the ability to control their emotions rather than their emotions controlling them.

> *"I realized that nobody's perfect. In a way it was such news to me because I'd been in an adult world, and there are such adult expectations to be perfect about everything. And you know, you don't have to be."*

Monica Seles

EMOTIONAL THREAT VS. EMOTIONAL CHALLENGE

In recent years, I have found that a simple distinction appears to to lie the Emotional racers have to their skiing: threat vs. challenge. At the heart of emotional threat is the perception that winning is all-important and failure is unacceptable. Emotional threat is most often associated with too great an emphasis on winning, results, and rankings. Pressure to win from parents, coaches, and racers themselves is also common. With these beliefs, it is easy to see why competing in ski racing would be emotionally threatening.

Emotional threat manifests itself in a negative "emotional chain" in which each link separately and cumulatively makes racers feel badly and hurts their skiing. The most common reaction to a threat is the desire to avoid the threat. There is often a loss of motivation to ski and compete, especially when the threat of losing is immediate, for example, when a racer is behind after the first run, (think of giving up as a major loss of motivation). Emotional threat also suggests to racers that they're incapable of overcoming the situation that is causing the threat, so their confidence is hurt and racers are overwhelmed with negative and defeatist thoughts.

The threat produces strong negative emotions such as fear, anger, frustration, depression, despair, and helplessness.

The emotional threat also causes anxiety and all of the negative physical symptoms associated with overintensity. The previous links in the emotional chain make it nearly impossible to focus effectively because there are so many negative things pulling racers' focus away from a useful process focus. All of the previous links in the chain ultimately result in very poor skiing and little enjoyment in ski racing.

In contrast, emotional challenge is associated with racers enjoying the process of ski racing regardless of whether they win or lose. The emphasis is on having fun and seeing racing as exciting and enriching. Ski racing, when seen as an emotional challenge, is an experience that is relished and sought out at every opportunity. Thus, emotional challenge is highly motivating, to the point where racers love competing in big races.

Emotional challenge communicates to racers that they have the ability to meet the demands of ski racing, so they're confident and filled with positive thoughts. Emotional challenge generates many positive emotions such as excitement, joy, and satisfaction. It also stimulates racers' bodies to achieve prime intensity, where their bodies are relaxed, energized, and physically capable of performing their best. Racers also have the ability to attain prime focus, in which they're totally focused on what enables them to ski their best. All of these links in the emotional challenge chain lead racers to Prime Ski Racing and great enjoyment in their ski racing.

"Emotionally it was my best program ever."

Tara Lipinski after winning 1996 Olympic skating gold medal

EMOTIONAL STYLES

I have found four emotional styles among racers. These styles involve characteristic ways in which racers respond emotionally to their skiing.

Racers with a particular style react in a predictable way any time they find themselves in a threatening situation.

The *seether* feels frustration and anger build slowly during the course of the race season. They appear to be in emotional control, but that is only because the negative emotions haven't surfaced yet. They're able to keep the frustration and anger in check as long as they are skiing well and the race season is mostly going their way. If the season turns on them or they have a particularly bad race, they can explode and lose control emotionally.

The *rager* also feels anger and frustration strongly, but it is expressed immediately and openly. For this type of racer, showing strong emotions acts as a form of relief. The emotions arise, are expressed, and released. By doing this, the rager is able to maintain a kind of emotional equilibrium. Up to a point, this ongoing emotional outlet helps their skiing by increasing motivation and intensity. However, though these racers let the negative emotions out, they do not really let them go. If they have a bad race, the rage builds until it finally engulfs and controls them. At this point, their emotions become their enemies and their skiing deteriorates.

The *brooder* also feel strong emotions, but, unlike the seether and the rager, the most common emotions are despair and helplessness. These racers tend to dwell on negative experiences, thoughts, and feelings and can be seen as pouting after a poor race. Brooders are very sensitive to the highs and lows of the race season and their emotions tend to mirror its course. If they're skiing well and having good results, they're fine, but if they ski poorly and have poor results, the "down" emotions emerge and impact their skiing. They possess a strong defeatist attitude and are best known for their giving up in pressure situations. There are no World Cup racers who completely fit this emotional style because someone could not reach such a high level of ski racing if their dominant emotional style was as a brooder. However, there are many racers at the highest level who have some brooding qualities.

The *zen master* is the rarest of the emotional styles because they're largely unaffected by threat and negative emotions. As if they're covered in teflon, mistakes, poor races, and losing seem to slide right off of them. They have the ability to not let pressure situations affect them and they're able to let go of past mistakes and failure. The zen master rarely shows emotions, either negative or positive, and maintains a consistent demeanor even in the most critical race situations.

What emotional style best describes you? Think back to races you have skied in that did not go well. How did you respond emotionally? Were you a seether, rager, brooder, or zen master? It's likely that a pattern of emotional reactions will emerge in your skiing that place you into one of the four emotional styles.

Emotional styles are not easy to change. In fact, there is some evidence that we are born with a particular temperament and we are "hard-wired" that way. If this is true, then it is difficult to change your emotional style. The goal then is not to alter your basic emotional response to the world, but instead to master your emotional style so that it helps rather than hurts your skiing.

> *"I don't get real emotional. Whatever happens, good or*
> *bad, I have to keep the same attitude."*
>
> ### NBA player Mike Bibby

EMOTIONAL MASTER OR VICTIM

Many racers believe that they have little control of their emotions and there is nothing they can do to gain control. If their emotions hurt them, they just have to accept it because they can't do anything about it. I call these racers *emotional victims*, where their emotions have total control over them, they possess unhealthy and unproductive emotional habits, and their emotions interfere with their happiness and their ability to ski well and succeed.

Despite these perceptions, my work has clearly shown that racers are capable of becoming *emotional masters*. Racers can gain control of their emotions. They can develop healthy and productive emotional habits. Their emotions can facilitate their happiness and their ability to succeed.

Emotions are a simple, but not easy, choice. They are a simple choice because if racers have the option to feel badly and ski poorly or feel good and ski well, they will certainly choose the latter option. However, emotions are not an easy choice because past emotional baggage and old emotional habits lead racers to respond emotionally in the present in ways that are unhealthy and result in poor skiing. The choice comes with awareness of when old emotional habits will arise and choosing a positive emotional response that will lead to good feelings and successful races.

> *"Emotion is what makes me what I am today. It makes me play bigger than I am."*
>
> **Charles Barkley**

RESPONDING TO FRUSTRATION

Frustration is at the heart of every negative emotional reaction. Frustration, in its most basic form, is the emotional reaction to racers' efforts toward a goal being thwarted. In other words, if their goal is to ski well and have a successful race, then racers may experience frustration if they're making mistakes, skiing poorly, or having poor results.

Frustration can initially be motivating because it pushes racers to find a way to remove the obstacles to their goal. If they're unable to turn their skiing around, then the initial frustration will become more persistent and stronger. Depending on their emotional style, racers will either begin to experience anger or despair. If further efforts go unrewarded, then the negative emotions will likely take over and they will get caught in the negative emotional chain I spoke of earlier.

If racers can learn to respond positively to frustration when it first occurs, they can prevent other stronger negative emotions from arising and they can stop the negative emotional chain before it starts. Their goal is to react positively to the first indication of negative emotions. This reaction starts with developing a positive attitude about the things that lead to frustration such as mistakes and poor results. It means making a shift from an attitude of emotional threat to one of emotional challenge.

Emotional threat is the primary cause of frustration in response to mistakes. Remember that for racers who experience emotional threat, failure of any sort is unacceptable. The threat response to frustration causes racers to dwell on the past. They continue to worry about mistakes and poor results even though there is nothing they can do about the past. These racers also ski scared because they're afraid of having to face what they perceive as failure. What they don't realize is that this attitude makes it more likely that they will make mistakes, ski poorly, and have poor results because they put great pressure on themselves to be perfect. Racers who ski under emotional threat are also emotional victims who feel helpless to do anything about how they feel and can be expected to ski their worst in important races.

Yet, failure, in the form of mistakes and poor results is a normal and inevitable part of ski racing. The best racers in the world ski poorly and lose races. Other racers must accept that they will also ski poorly and they will have some poor results. These "failures" do not make racers failures. Even if racers make mistakes and ski poorly, they can still be good racers who ski well and are successful most of the time. With this emotional challenge attitude, racers can unburden themselves of the unrealistic pressure that they must ski perfectly and have great results every time they race. With this weight off their shoulders, mistakes and losses will no longer be a threat and will be less likely to trigger frustration.

Changing this attitude where failure is unacceptable requires that racers alter their goal for their ski racing. Most racers who have an attitude of emotional threat have perfection as their goal. Racers who strive for perfection will continue to experience frustration and the negative emotional chain because they will never achieve the unrealistic and unattainable goal of perfection.

A healthier and more reasonable goal is excellence, which I define as *skiing well most of the time.* The goal of excellence still sets a high standard of racing, but it also allows the possibility and acceptance of mistakes and poor skiing. Excellence relieves the pressure of having to be perfect and never making mistakes or skiing poorly.

With this emotional challenge attitude in place, you're in a position to take practical steps to counter the frustration you will periodically experience. First, you can learn to identify when frustration usually begins for you. Frustration typically occurs in response to a pattern of mistakes or poor races. Perhaps it is after you have made the same mistake three times or have had two bad races in a row. The next step is to recognize a pattern before frustration arises. If you make the same mistake several times in a row, for example, you keep hooking tips in slalom, you know that if you repeat the mistake you will become frustrated. It's also important to stay focused on the present rather than dwelling on past mistakes. Having realized that frustration is just around the corner, you can find a solution to the problem so the pattern doesn't continue. For example, make a technical or tactical correction that will enable you to stop hooking tips.

Also, realize that you have the opportunity to be an emotional master rather than an emotional victim. As an emotional master, you can choose how you will react to your skiing. You can choose to feel badly and ski poorly or opt to feel good and ski better. In fact, how quickly you make the choice in response to frustration will determine how long you continue to ski poorly and whether you ultimately win or lose races. The sooner you make the right choice, the sooner you can raise your skiing and have a chance to win.

"I can maintain a level head when I make huge mistakes. I don't get down on myself between turns or when something goes wrong, or in a larger sense between runs or races."

USST member Bode Miller

EMOTIONAL MASTERY

The process of emotional mastery begins with recognizing the negative emotional reactions that hurt your skiing. When you start to feel negative emotions before a race, be aware of what they are, for instance, frustration, anger, or depression. Then identify what situation caused them.

After the race, consider what was the underlying cause of the emotions. This might require you to examine your emotional baggage. If the emotions are strong and you find that they present themselves in other parts of your life, you might consider seeking professional help. Such guidance can assist you in better understanding your emotional habits, how they may interfere with many aspects of your life, and how you can learn new emotional responses that will better serve you in your ski racing and in your life.

To continue the process of emotional mastery in training and races, specify alternative emotional reactions to the situations that commonly trigger negative emotions. For example, instead of yelling, "I am terrible," you could slap your thigh and say, "Come on, better next time." This positive emotional response will help you let go of the past mistakes, motivate you to ski better next time, generate positive emotions that will give you more confidence, and allow you to focus on what will help you raise the level of your skiing.

Recalling that mental skills like emotional mastery are skills, this positive reaction will not be easy at first because your negative emotional habits are well ingrained. With training and the realization that you feel better and your skiing improves with a positive response, you will, in time, retrain your emotions into a positive emotional habit.

> *"Crossing the finish line always brings a gut-check sensation of either a really good emotional surge or the opposite–negative agitation."*

> **Sarah Schleper**

SECTION IV:

PRIME SKI RACING SKILLS

CHAPTER SEVEN:

PRIME SKI RACING TRAINING

As my first law of preparation indicates, races aren't won on race day, but rather in the days, weeks, and months leading up to the race. What racers do in training will determine how they ski and the ultimate outcome of the race. Training is where the development of Prime Ski Racing begins. It's the place where all of the physical, technical, tactical, and mental requirements of ski racing are established.

Despite this importance, I'm constantly amazed by the poor quality of training in which I see racers engage, even at the world-class level. I see poor effort, ineffective focus, and little intensity. Yet these racers expect to ski their best in races. That's unlikely to happen because they're not engaging in prime training. Prime training involves maintaining the highest level of effort, focus, and intensity consistently throughout a training session. Without prime training, Prime Ski Racing will never be achieved.

> *"Every time I train I go beyond my limit, that way when I put on the 'race face,' I know I am prepared to win."*
>
> **Sarah Schleper**

Positive Change Formula

Change of any sort, whether physical, technical, tactical, or mental, doesn't occur automatically. There is a three-step process that will enable you to develop your Prime Ski Racing skills in the quickest and most efficient way possible. I call it the Positive Change Formula (see below). First, you have to become aware of what you're doing incorrectly and how to improve it. Second, you need to control what you want to improve. Finally, you must put in the necessary repetition to ingrain the positive changes fully. Developing your Prime Ski Racing skills involves an awareness of your physical, technical, tactical, and mental states, taking active steps to control them, and doing sufficient repetition to make the changes automatic. This process produces positive change, which leads to Prime Ski Racing.

POSITIVE CHANGE FORMULA

Awareness + Control + Repetition = POSITIVE CHANGE

Prime Ski Racing Training

Too often, I see racers begin training without any clear idea of what they're doing there. They have nothing in particular they're working on and so they aren't working on anything specific to improve. When this happens, racers are not only not improving, they're also making it more difficult to improve because they're ingraining old and ineffective skills, which makes it harder to learn new skills.

Goal and purpose. To prevent this, you need to always train with a goal and a purpose. A goal is some aspect of your ski racing that you want to improve. It might be physical, technical, tactical, or mental. A purpose is something specific you work on during training that will enable you to achieve your goal. For example, if a racer's goal is to maintain a lower tuck on the flats, his purpose would be to lower his hips and feel his chest against his thighs. Every time you go to training, you should have a goal and a purpose. If you don't, you'll be getting better at getting worse.

100% focus and intensity. Another area most racers need to work on is their focus and intensity in training. As my fifth law of preparation suggests, racers want to train at a level of focus and intensity that will allow them to ski their best in races. Racers will ski in races at the level of focus and intensity at which they train. Ideally, racers should ski at 100% focus and intensity. As I indicated in Chapters Four and Five, racers have unique intensity and focus styles in which they ski their best. When I talk about 100% focus and intensity, I mean training at or near the level of focus and intensity that allows racers to ski their best.

Too often I see racers training at a level much different than the level at which they want to race. When they're free skiing, they may be at 70% focus and intensity. In training, they may up their focus and intensity to 80%. When they get to a race, they want to ski at 100%. When they try to do this, one of two things happens. Since they've been training at 70% to 80% focus and intensity, that's what comes out in the race. Or they try to ski at 100% focus and intensity, but since they haven't trained at that level, their skiing actually gets worse rather than better. In either case, the result is that they don't ski their best.

Train for adversity. As I suggested in Chapter Three with respect to confidence, an essential skill that racers need to develop to ski their best is responding positively to adversity. Most racers like to train in ideal conditions, but conditions are rarely perfect in races. Too often in training, I see racers put forth less effort or stop completely when the conditions get too difficult, for example, the course get rutted out. Racers will say it doesn't matter since it's just training. But racers don't realize two things. What racers do in training is what they will do in races. If racers give up in training when things get too tough, then they're becoming skilled at giving up in the face of adversity. It is often how racers respond to adversity that determines who wins the race. The reality is that difficult conditions occur for all racers, so your competition also has to deal with them. What makes the difference in a race is who responds to the adversity best.

The only way to learn to race in adverse conditions is to train in them. This skill comes from accepting that the conditions will interfere with your ability to ski your best and also realizing that your competition must deal with them as well. Learning to respond positively to adversity comes from realizing that you probably won't ski your best in difficult conditions. What you may not realize is that you don't have to ski well to win. You only need to ski better than your competition. By training for adversity, you come to understand the adverse conditions and you learn how to adapt yourself to them. By training for adversity, you develop the skills so that your skiing doesn't deteriorate too much due to the tough conditions.

Responding positively to adversity also comes from being determined not to let the adversity beat you. A part of this is the ability to accept that you will make more mistakes and to not allow yourself to become frustrated because your skiing declines. You must stay positive and motivated even when things get tough. Having trained for adversity, when you race in adverse conditions, you can say, "I've been training in these conditions. I know what to do to ski well. This is no big deal."

The value of mistakes. Perhaps the most frustrating part of ski racing is all the mistakes you make as you develop as a racer. Most racers view mistakes as failure. Racers often see mistakes as a personal attack on their ability as a racer and their worth as a person. As I described in Chapter Six, for many racers, making mistakes is unacceptable and a source of frustration and other negative emotions.

Most racers don't realize that the best racers in the world make mistakes all of the time. What makes these racers great is not that they don't make mistakes, but rather it is the attitude they have about their mistakes and how they respond to those they do make. Mistakes only mean failure if racers don't learn from them and if they keep repeating them.

Mistakes are a natural and necessary part of becoming a better ski racer. They really mean that racers are becoming more successful because they're moving out of their comfort zone. Mistakes mean racers are working to improve. They are also valuable information showing racers what they need to work on. If racers aren't making mistakes, they're not pushing themselves to become a better ski racer. Mistakes indicate that racers are taking risks, going for it, and doing something new. Mistakes mean success when racers learn from them and they stop repeating them.

What is ironic is that most racers' attitudes toward mistakes actually increase the likelihood that they will continue. By getting frustrated and discouraged, racers are more likely to make more mistakes because they become tentative, doubtful, anxious, and focused on failure. Learning from their mistakes, and not repeating them, involves racers knowing how to respond to the mistakes they make. Racers need to learn to respond in a positive and constructive way.

The goal is to reduce the number of mistakes you make in training by figuring out how to correct them and ingraining the proper execution. The first step is to identify what you're doing wrong that is causing the mistake. For example, a racer keeps sliding below the best line for a course. Next, you can specify what you need to do to correct the problem. In the case of the racer, he may need to start his turn earlier and finish the turn before he passes the gate. Then, when you prepare for your next run, you can focus on the correction, which should solve the problem that's leading to the mistake being repeated.

Get out of your comfort zone. Most racers like to stay in their comfort zone. They like to ski the way they usually do and they get uncomfortable if they try to do anything differently. This approach might make them feel good, but the problem is that they'll never ski their best or move up to a new level.

To become your best, you must move out of your comfort zone. This means making changes to your skiing that will enable you to ski faster in the future. For example, a racer is uncomfortable catching air in downhills.

Whenever there is big air on a downhill course, he would stand up and minimize the air he caught. But if he wants to become a good downhiller, he must learn to carry speed over bumps, which means sometimes catching a lot of air. The risk of moving out of your comfort zone is that you'll make some mistakes at first and might ski poorly for a while. But as you do it more, you become more skilled and familiar with it, until you reach a point at which it's no longer uncomfortable. Before you know it, you've raised your comfort zone and your skiing to a new level.

Never give up. There's a tendency among many racers to give up in training when they're not skiing well. They might ski out when they get into trouble. They rationalize giving up by saying that training doesn't really count for anything. My twelve laws of preparation would argue otherwise. Training matters because everything racers practice either contributes to or interferes with developing effective competitive skills and habits.

If racers give up in training, they're learning the skill of giving up. If racers practice giving up in training, when they ski poorly in a race, their learned skill will be to give up. The skill of never giving up is so important because something rather important happens every time racers give up: They automatically lose. If racers keep fighting, they may not win, but at least they have a chance. Racers want to ingrain the skill of skiing at 100% and never giving up no matter what happens during training or a race.

> *"It's doing more than everyone else. It's finding your own way to make your body tough, and fit. It's the extra two reps in the weight room. It's an extra interval."*
>
> **Sarah Schleper**

CHAPTER EIGHT:

PRIME SKI RACING ROUTINES

Routines are one of the most important aspects of ski racing that racers can develop to improve their training and competitive performances. The fundamental value of routines is that they ensure total preparation in racers' efforts. Routines enable racers to be completely physically, technically, tactically, and mentally ready to ski their best. I don't know a world-class athlete in any sport who does not use routines in some part of his or her competitive preparations.

Routines are most often used before races to make sure that racers are prepared to ski their best. Routines can also be developed in training to ensure that racers get the most out of their training time.

There are a lot of things in ski racing that racers can't control such as weather and snow conditions. Ultimately, the only thing racers can control is themselves. Routines can increase their control over their skiing by enabling racers to directly prepare every area that impacts their skiing. Those areas racers can control include their equipment (is your gear in optimal condition?), their body (are you physically and technically warmed up?), and their mind (are you at prime focus and intensity?).

Routines also allow racers to make their preparation more predictable by knowing they're systematically covering every area that will influence their skiing. Racers can also expect the unexpected. In other words, they can plan for every eventuality that could arise at a race. If racers can reduce the things that can go wrong and be prepared for those things that do, they'll be better able to stayed focused and relaxed before and during the races.

All of your preparations involves a consistent narrowing of effort, energy, and focus. Each step closer to the race should lead you to that unique state of readiness in which you are physically and mentally ready to ski your best. You can think of your preparation as a funnel. Whatever you put into the funnel will dictate what comes out. If you put good preparation into the funnel, what will come out is good skiing. I call this the Prime Ski Racing Funnel.

Some sport psychologists use the term, ritual, in place of routine. I don't like this term because it has connotations that go against what routines are trying to accomplish. Remember, the goal of routines is to totally prepare racers for training and races. Everything done in a routine serves a specific and practical function in that readiness process. For example, a physical warm-up for a race is essential for total preparation.

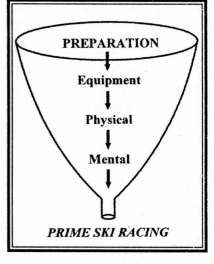

In contrast, a ritual is associated with superstitions and is often made up of things that have no practical impact on races, for instance, wearing lucky socks or following a specific route to the hill. Routines can also be adjusted should the need arise, for example, if you arrive late to the race, you can shorten your routine and still get prepared. Rituals, though, are rigid and ceremonial. Racers can believe that rituals must be done or they will not ski well. You control routines, but rituals control you.

"If you succeed in a race while wearing a certain pair of undertrousers one day, and then you wear the same undertrousers day after day, you may still succeed, but it will not be because of the undertrousers."

Kjetil Andre Aamodt

BENEFITS OF RACE ROUTINES

Routines have many benefits to training and racing. Foremost, they develop consistency in all areas that impact ski racing. By consistently going through their routine, racers are training their mind and body to respond the same way regardless of the situation. As my seventh law of preparation suggests, consistent preparation leads to consistent thinking, intensity, focus, emotions, and physical and technical readiness, which will result in Prime Ski Racing.

At the same time, consistency does not mean rigidity. Routines are flexible. They can be adjusted to different situations that arise, for example, a delay in the start of a race. Flexibility in routines means racers won't be surprised or stressed by changes that occur during their preparations. Flexibility means racers will be better able to ski their best in a wider range of race situations and conditions. Ultimately, the goal of routines in training and races is to ensure that when racers leave the starting gate, they're totally physically, technically, tactically, and mentally prepared to ski their best.

"To repeat successes of the past, you follow your old program. Don't get fancy; just be consistent."

Former Olympic marathoner Bill Rodgers

Training Routines

Developing routines should begin in training. For you to get the most out of your training, you should develop a brief training routine that will ensure that you're totally prepared for every training run. The first step in your training routine is getting your body ready. This involves checking and adjusting your intensity as needed. This might mean taking deep breaths to calm yourself down or using intense breaths to raise your intensity. I recommend that before every training run, you jump up and down to get your body going in preparation for the start of the run. Second, you need to focus on what you want to work on during the run. If you have an internal focus style, your Mag-Lite® beam should already be narrow and focused on a particular cue. If you have an external focus style, this would be the time to narrow your beam onto the cue. To narrow your focus, you can remind yourself what is the purpose of the training run. Then, you can repeat your keyword. At this point when you begin your run, your body and your mind are ready to ski your best.

Your training routine need only last a few seconds, but will completely prepare you to get the most out of your training. It will also lay the foundation for using routines before races. Remember, for your training routine to become effective, you must use it every time you take a training run.

> *"I think training's just like racing. I want to go out there and pretend it's a race day every day. That way, when I get to a race, it's no big deal."*
>
> **USST member Erik Schlopy**

Pre-Race Routines

The next step in developing effective race routines is to create a pre-race routine that is an extended version of the training routine. The goal is the same, to be totally prepared to ski your best. The difference is that a pre-race routine will dictate how you ski in your upcoming race and it can take up to several hours to complete.

There is no one ideal routine for everyone. Pre-race routines are individual. For every great racer, you'll see a different routine, but all will have common elements. You have to decide what exactly to put into your routine and how to structure it. Developing an effective pre-race routine is a progressive process that will take time before you have one that really works for you.

Prime start. One of the first lessons that emerged from my work with World Cup racers was that they could not afford to work their way into a race run. It is not uncommon for racers from weekend warriors to juniors to national team racers to believe that they can take the first few gates to settle into their race run and then really turn it on. But these racers seem to forget that the clock starts when they leave the starting gate. If racers are not going for it from the moment they trip the wand, they are falling behind and having to play catch up the rest of the run. In a sense, racers are making a fundamental mistake; they are using the beginning of their race run as a warm-up. In ski racing, where races are won and lost by hundredths of a second, this approach will not work.

If you're racing against a weak field that you are better than, then you can fall behind and once you get going, you'll be able to catch up and still win the race. However, these races are not why you're striving to achieve Prime Ski Racing. The real meaning of experiencing Prime Ski Racing is that you're competing against a tough field of competitors who are as good or better than you in a race that matters. In this kind of race, a slow start will guarantee a poor result. Once you fall behind in the first few gates, you will not be able to catch back up.

Having a prime start depends on being totally prepared to ski your best from the very start of the race. Your ability to experience a prime start is based on whether you're physically, technically, tactically, and mentally ready to achieve Prime Ski Racing from the moment you leave the starting gate.

At the heart of this readiness is your pre-race routine. It should ensure that you are completely ready to ski at your highest level from the start of your race run. There are several key components to making sure this happens. First, you must have a good physical warm-up. If your body is not prepared, you will not be able to have a prime start to the race. Your physical warm-up should include everything necessary to ensure total physical readiness. Common physical warm-up activities in ski racing include a short run, jumping rope, stretching, and agility drills. This part of the pre-race routine will also help you move toward your prime intensity.

The next step in your pre-race preparations should be your skiing warm-up. This is a process by which you simulate turns for the event in which you are competing with increasing focus and intensity until you are confident and comfortable. This is an area where I see many racers fall short. Most skiing warm-ups I see are unstructured and unfocused, in which racers half-heartedly and incompletely get themselves warmed up on their skis.

A skiing warm-up that leads to a prime start should include both free skiing and training course warm-up. It should be organized and comprehensive, systematically moving you toward race readiness. Your skiing warm-up should begin with relaxed and comfortable skiing, allowing your body to warm up, and then increase in energy and effort. The last part of the free skiing and training course warm-ups should be performed with race focus and intensity. This step enables you to leave the starting gate and make your first race turn with absolute physical confidence, comfort, and quality.

The final step of the prime start warm-up is mental. You should check and adjust your focus and intensity. You can also preview your race run using imagery in which you review your line and ingrain the image and feeling of skiing fast. Having engaged in the process of a prime start, when you leave the starting gate and your race run begins, you can ski to your fullest ability and ensure that you will be competitive from the moment you kick the wand.

Focus needs. The goal in your pre-race routine if you have an internal focus style is to put yourself in a place where there are few external distractions and where you can focus on your pre-race preparation. To maintain that narrow Mag-Lite® beam, you want to go through your pre-race routine away from other people and activities that could distract you.

An external focus style means that you need to keep your Mag-Lite® beam wide during your preparations so you can keep your mind off the upcoming race and away from thinking too much. The goal in your pre-race routine if you have an external focus style is to put yourself in a place where you're unable to become focused internally and think about the race. Your pre-race routine should be done where there is enough activity to draw your focus away from inside your head. To widen the beam, you want to go through your pre-race routine around people and activities that can draw your focus outward.

Intensity needs. You'll also want to build your pre-race routine around your intensity needs. The intensity component of your pre-race routine should include checking your intensity periodically before the approaching race and using psych-up or psych-down techniques to adjust it as needed. You'll need to set aside time in your routine when you can do these techniques. As you approach the start of the race, you'll want to move closer to your prime intensity. The short period just before your start should be devoted to a final check and adjustment of your intensity.

If you ski best at a lower level of intensity, you want your pre-race routine to be done at an easy pace and have plenty of opportunities take a break to slow down and relax. You'll want to be around people who are relaxed and low-key as well. If you're around anxious people, they'll make you nervous too.

If you ski best at a higher level of intensity, you want your pre-race routine to be done at a faster pace with more energy put into the components of your routine. You will want to make sure that you are constantly doing something. There should be little time during which you are just standing around and waiting. You'll also want to be around people who are energetic and outgoing.

Music. Music is a powerful tool you can use to assist in your pre-race preparations. It can help you achieve both prime focus and prime intensity. Music can also positively impact your emotions. Listening to music can help you adjust your Mag-Lite® beam. You can use music as a way of narrowing your Mag-Lite® beam by drawing your focus away from what is happening around you. If you're focused on your music, you won't be paying attention to your surroundings. Music is also a way for you to widen your Mag-Lite® beam by drawing your focus outside of your head. If you're listening to music, you're less likely to be thinking too much about your competition.

As I discussed in Chapter Four, music can have a similar impact on your intensity. We all know how powerful music can be. Music has the ability to soothe us or get us fired up. In this way, you can use music to help adjust your intensity. If you need to lower your intensity, you should listen to calming music. If you need to raise your intensity, you should listen to high-energy music.

You can also use music to alter your emotions. Music has the power to inspire us, to excite us, or to make us sad or angry. By listening to the right kind of music, you can actively create the emotions you want to ski your best. For example, hard rock will energize and motivate you or classical music will make you feel happy and content.

> *"My best races this year have consisted of a good mental warm-up."*
>
> **Sarah Schleper**

DESIGNING A PRE-RACE ROUTINE

The first step in designing a pre-race routine is to make a list of everything you need to do before a race to be prepared. Some of the common elements you should include are meals, physical warm-up, technical warm-up, inspection, equipment check, and mental preparation. Other more personal things that might go into a pre-race routine include going to the bathroom and using mental imagery.

Then, decide in what order you want to do the components of your list as you approach the start of the race. In doing this, consider race activities that might need to be taken into account. For instance, length of time it takes to ride the life to the start and the availability of training courses on which to warm up can influence when you accomplish different parts of your pre-race routine.

Next, specify where each step of your routine can best be completed. You should use your knowledge of race sites at which you often ski to figure this part out. For example, if you like to be alone before a race, is there a place near the start area where you can get away from people?

Finally, establish a time frame and a schedule for completing your routine. In other words, how much time do you need to get totally prepared? Some racers like to get to the start area only a short time before their start. Others like to arrive 45 minutes before. All of these decisions are personal. You need to find out what works best for you. Use the Personalized Pre-Race Routine form (see page 117) to assist you in developing your pre-race routine.

Once your pre-race routine is organized, try it out at races. Some things may work and others may not. In time, you'll be able to fine-tune your routine until you find the one that's most comfortable and best prepares you for a race. Lastly, remember, pre-race routines only have value if they're used consistently. If you use your routine before every race, in a short time, you won't even have to think about doing it. Your pre-race routine will simply be what you do before each race and it will ensure that you are totally prepared to ski your best.

> *"The key to race day is to be on your own program, doing the things that matter the most for you."*

Sarah Schleper

PERSONALIZED PRE-RACE ROUTINE

Directions: List the pre-race activities that will help you to totally prepare to ski your best.

Early in Day

      1.   Physical:

      2.   Mental:

At Race Site

      1.   Physical:

      2.   Mental:

Final Preparation

      1.   Equipment:

      2.   Physical:

      3.   Mental:

CHAPTER NINE:

PRIME SKI RACING IMAGERY

Race imagery is one of the most powerful tools racers can use to improve their ski racing. It's used by virtually all great racers and there is considerable scientific research supporting its value. This research indicates that using race imagery alone produces gains in performance. More importantly, combining actual training with race imagery results in more improvement than training alone.

Race imagery is so beneficial because it impacts every contributor to Prime Ski Racing. It improves every part of the Prime Ski Racing pyramid. Race imagery increases motivation by allowing racers to see and feel themselves working hard and reaching their goals. It builds confidence by enabling racers to see and feel themselves skiing fast and succeeding. Race imagery improves intensity by allowing racers to imagine experiencing pressure and using psych-up or psych-down techniques to control it. It enhances focus by identifying important cues and letting racers rehearse prime focus. Finally, race imagery enables racers to generate positive emotions in response to seeing and feeling themselves ski their best.

Race imagery also improves technical, tactical, and competitive development. It ingrains the image and feeling of correct technique and provides imagined repetition of proper execution. Race imagery also enables racers to further learn sound tactics and instill effective competitive skills, habits, and routines. Finally, it ingrains the image and feeling of racers skiing their best.

Race imagery can be used in several settings that will help racers achieve Prime Ski Racing. During training, racers can use it to facilitate their technical development and improve the quality of their training. On race day, racers can use race imagery as part of their pre-race routine.

> *"If I'm nervous, I will mentally run the course over and over, but if I'm not nervous, I just go over it once or twice."*
>
> **Picabo Street**

RACE IMAGERY IS A SKILL

It's important to understand that race imagery is a skill, just like a technical skill, that develops with practice. Few racers have perfect race imagery when they first use it. It's common for racers who haven't used race imagery before to struggle with it at first. This discourages them and leads them to believe that race imagery can't be beneficial. If racers put in the time and effort, their race imagery will improve and it will become a valuable tool for them.

The first thing you want to do is assess your imagery abilities. To do this, complete the Ski Racing Imagery Profile (see page 121). It will give a graphic representation of your race imagery strengths and areas in need of improvement. Using this information, you can emphasize and strengthen the areas in need of work in your race imagery program. The next section will describe each factor in more detail and provide exercises to improve each imagery area.

> *"I'm visualizing every single part of the downhill course. I want it to be totally rehearsed in my head."*
>
> **Chad Fleischer**

RACE IMAGERY FACTORS

Perspective—Internal imagery (from inside your body looking out) or external imagery (from outside your body like watching yourself on video) or both. (1-all internal; 5-both; 10-all external)

Control—Control of your images as you ski (e.g., ski well with an accurate image of how you ski or difficulty imagining how you ski or making mistakes in your imagery). (1-no control; 10-total control)

Visual—How clearly you see yourself skiing (e.g., see all aspects of skiing). (1-unclear; 10-clear)

Auditory—How clearly you hear sounds associated with skiing (e.g., skis on snow, hitting gates). (1-unclear; 10-clear)

Physical feeling—How clearly you feel yourself skiing (e.g., muscles working, pressure on bottom of feet). (1-unclear; 10-clear)

Thoughts—How well you are able to reproduce the thoughts that you have when you are skiing (e.g., about technique, tactics, positive or negative). (1-no thoughts; 10-usual thoughts)

Emotions—How well you are able to reproduce the emotions that you feel when you are skiing (e.g., excitement, frustration, anger, depression). (1-no emotions; 10-strong emotions)

Total image—How well you are able to accurately reproduce the race experience (e.g., all of the senses, thoughts, emotions, and physical feelings). (1-poor reproduction; 10-exact reproduction)

Speed—Your ability to speed up or slow down your imagery. (1-not at all; 10-easily)

RACE IMAGERY PROFILE

Name _____   **Date** _____

Directions: Nine factors that are important for race imagery are identified in the profile below. Before rating yourself on each factor, close your eyes and imagine skiing for 30 seconds, paying attention to a particular factor. Indicate how you perceive yourself on the 1-10 scale for each factor by drawing a line at that rating number and shading in the area toward the center of the profile. Except for Perspective, a score below a 7 indicates an area in need of improvement.

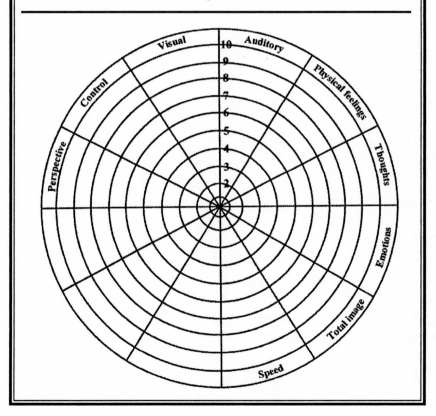

Maximizing Race Imagery

There are seven factors that will impact the quality of your race imagery: perspective, control, multiple sense, thoughts, emotions, total image, and speed. Each of these areas can be developed with training.

Imagery perspective. Imagery perspective refers to where the "imagery camera" is when you do race imagery. You will use one of two perspectives. The internal perspective involves seeing yourself from inside your body looking out, as if you were actually skiing. The imagery camera is inside your head looking out through your eyes. The external perspective involves seeing yourself from outside your body like on video. The imagery camera follows your skiing from the outside.

Research indicates that one perspective is not better than the other. Rather, most people have a dominant perspective with which they're most comfortable. There are also some people who are equally adept at both perspectives. You should use the perspective that's most natural for you and then experiment with the other perspective to see if it helps you in a different way.

Try this exercise. Imagine yourself skiing four time for 30 seconds. The first two times use your dominant perspective. The next two times use the other perspective. You may find that only one perspective works for you or you may find that you can use either perspective equally well. In either case, for the time being, rely on the perspective that comes most naturally to you.

Control. Have you ever been doing race imagery and you keep making mistakes, for example, you keep hooking tips or falling in your imagery? This problem relates to imagery control, which is how well you're able to imagine what you want to imagine. It's not uncommon for racers new to race imagery to ski poorly in their imagery. This can be frustrating because if you can't imagine good skiing in your head, you're probably going to have a difficult time skiing well in real life.

You may find that the amount of imagery control you have depends on which event you imagine yourself skiing in. In general, you will have the most imagery control in events in which you are most skilled and most confident and you will have the least control in events in which you aren't very good and lack confidence. For example, if slalom is your worst event and you don't believe that you're a very good slalom skier, you will probably find that you will hook tips and ski out often in your race imagery.

Imagery control is a skill that develops with practice. If mistakes occur in your imagery, you shouldn't just let them go by. If you do, you'll ingrain the negative image and feeling which will hurt your skiing. Instead, when you ski poorly in your imagery, immediately rewind the "imagery video" and edit it. That is, rerun the imagery video until you do it correctly.

Try this exercise. Imagine yourself skiing five times for 30 seconds. In each segment, if you make a mistake, rewind and edit your imagery until you get it right. I've sometimes found it difficult for racers to edit their imagery when they imagine themselves skiing at full speed. It can be helpful when they're having difficulty controlling their imagery to slow their imagery down, in which they see and feel themselves skiing in slow motion. This technique seems to enable racers to have greater control of their imagery. As they gain better control of their imagery in slow motion, they can progressively increase the speed of their imagery while maintaining good control until they're able to ski well at "real time" speed.

Multiple senses. You may have noticed that I use the word imagery rather than visualization to describe this technique. This is because visualization places too much emphasis on its visual component. Good race imagery is more than just visual. The best imagery involves the multi-sensory reproduction of the actual skiing experience. You should see, hear, and feel your race imagery.

Visual imagery involves how clearly you see yourself skiing. Ideally, your visual images should be as clear as if you are actually skiing. It may be, though, that your images are blurry or you can't see yourself at all.

In order to imagine yourself skiing, you must know what you look like as a skier. If you can't produce an accurate image of how you ski, you will probably imagine yourself skiing like someone you ski with or like a World Cup racer. In either case, the images will not help you because they will be inconsistent with how you actually ski.

Try this exercise. Watch yourself skiing on video, then immediately close your eyes and reproduce the video images. As the visual image of how you ski becomes more clear, put away the video for a while and repeat the accurate visual images of your skiing. If the image starts to fade, return to the video until you're able to see yourself skiing consistently. This exercise will help you ingrain an accurate image of how you ski.

Vivid auditory images are important because sounds can play an important part in ski racing. For example, the sound of the skis on the snow tell you about the snow conditions.

Try this exercise. Imagine skiing three times for 30 seconds. Each time, focus on a different sound associated with skiing. Once you're able to do this consistently, put all of the sounds together and hear the various sounds in one sequence of race imagery.

I believe that the most powerful part of race imagery is feeling it in your body. That's how you really ingrain new technical and mental skills and habits. A useful way to increase the feeling in your race imagery is to combine imagined and real sensations. Imagine yourself skiing and move your body with the imagined skiing. By integrating the imagined sensations with the actual physical feelings, you can improve the value of race imagery even more.

Try this exercise. Imagine skiing two times for 30 seconds. Each time, focus on feeling your muscles and the physical movements. Then, imagine skiing two more times focusing on the feeling, but this time, move your body with the imagery to simulate the actual movement, for example, hands up and knees moving back and forth. By combining the imagined feelings with the actual physical feelings, you'll further enhance the quality of your race imagery and increase its benefits.

Thoughts. What you think before and during a race often dictates your intensity, emotions, and how you ski. Race imagery gives you the ability to learn new and better ways of thinking at races. You can generate race situations in your imagery in which you have displayed negative self-talk and body language. Drawing on the techniques described in Chapter Three, you can replace the negative self-talk and body language with positive expressions that will help you achieve Prime Ski Racing. Using race imagery in this way enables you to gain the added repetition of positive thinking that will further ingrain new positive thinking skills.

Try this exercise. Imagine yourself in a race in which you have negative self-talk and body language. Allow yourself to experience the negative thoughts and body language, then imagine yourself replacing the negatives with positive expressions using thought-stopping, positive keywords, and positive body language. Then, imagine yourself skiing well.

Emotions. Emotions play an important role in your ability to achieve Prime Ski Racing. Incorporating them into race imagery can be a valuable way to ingrain positive emotions into your skiing. Much like at actual races, imagining scenarios that have in the past evoked negative emotions gives you the opportunity to respond to them in an emotionally different way.

Try this exercise. Imagine yourself at a race in which you feel negative emotions, for example, you get frustrated when you make a mistake. Allow yourself to experience the frustration and then project yourself ahead and replace the negative emotions with positive ones that will help you ski better.

Total image. Another key aspect of race imagery is being able to imagine the total race performance. The most effective imagery reproduces every aspect of the actual race experience. In your race imagery, you should duplicate the sights, sounds, physical sensations, thoughts, and emotions that you would experience at an actual race.

Try this exercise. Imagine yourself skiing five times for 30 seconds. In each segment, choose a different aspect of a race to focus on, for example, visual, auditory, physical feeling, thoughts, and emotions. Emphasize experiencing that part of the race experience. Then, imagine skiing five more times. In this imagery, combine all the aspects of race imagery and imagine the total race performance. The more you can exactly reproduce the actual race experience, the more you'll get from your race imagery.

Speed. The ability to adjust the speed of your imagery will enable you to use race imagery to improve different aspects of your skiing. Slow motion is effective for focusing on technique. During actual training, it's difficult to work on technique at full speed. Instead, you begin technical change at slow speed under easy conditions. The same thing works for race imagery. When you first start to work on technique in your imagery, slow the imagery video down, frame by frame if necessary, to see yourself executing the skill correctly. Then slowly increase the speed of your imagery to "real time" until you're able to execute the technique at full speed.

You can use high-speed race imagery to improve your speed and reactions. Just as in actual training, thoughts and external distractions can interfere with your skiing. It can be difficult to maintain focus and rely on your reactions to ski well. Similarly, in imagery, thoughts can intrude and can hurt focus and the imagined skiing. Use fast motion imagery to develop better focus and to improve your reactions. Speed up your race imagery so you don't have time to be distracted. High-speed imagery reduces thinking, primes reactions, and hones automatic performance.

Try this exercise. Choose a technique you're working on in your skiing. Imagine using the technique six times. The first two times, slow down the imagery so you can really focus on doing it correctly. If you can do the technique properly at slow speed, increase the speed to a moderate rate. If you can do the technique correctly at a moderate speed, increase the imagery to full speed. You know you have the technique ingrained in your mind and body when you can do it correctly at high speed.

"I slip by each gate, visualizing myself at full speed busting through it. After visualizing myself skiing the entire course, I'm so ready to ski...that I can barely wait...for my start."

Sarah Schleper

RACE IMAGERY FOR PRIME TRAINING

There are several places you can incorporate race imagery into your training. Just before you begin a training run, instead of thinking about what you want to work on, see and feel yourself doing it with race imagery. Close your eyes and briefly imagine how you want to ski that run. This will increase your focus on the purpose of the training run and give you a positive image and feeling that will help its execution.

You can also use race imagery when you've finished a training run. If you just had a great run in which you skied well, the most important thing you want to do is remember the image and feeling. So right after the run, close your eyes and replay the run with race imagery. This will ingrain the positive image and feeling.

If you just had a poor training run in which you made mistakes, the dominant feeling and image is negative. The last thing you want to do is remember it. Yet, that is the image and feeling in your mind and body, and it is what will come out when you begin your next training run. You need to flush out the negative image and feeling. Right after the run, edit your race imagery, this time skiing well in the training run. This editing process clears out the negative image and feeling and replaces it with positive ones.

You can also use race imagery after your coach has given you instruction. Typically, a coach will give you feedback and then will tell you to think about it before you begin your next training run. But where does thinking occur? In your head. Where does skiing occur? In your body. Thinking about instruction doesn't always translate into the body effectively. Race imagery acts as a bridge between the thoughts in your mind and the actions in your body. You can use race imagery to ingrain the instruction into your mind and body. After your coach gives you instruction, close your eyes and imagine yourself making the correction that you were just told.

> *"I visualized GS for two weeks and then after a few runs, it was a breakthrough. I realized, I'm there, that's what it's supposed to feel like."*
>
> **Casey Puckett**

RACE IMAGERY FOR COMPETITION

Race imagery can be a valuable tool before races. As a part of your pre-race routine, you can use imagery in several places before your race run. You can use race imagery as part of your inspection. Race imagery can be useful for memorizing the course completely. Also, instead of thinking about the line you want to take, imagine yourself skiing that line. As you ride the lift before your race run, you can use race imagery to further memorize and ingrain how you want to ski the course. Finally, when you arrive at the start area, you can use race imagery to build confidence with good imagined skiing and to generate prime focus and intensity before your race run.

> *"Before a jump, I'll rock back and forth, close my eyes and envision the perfect jump."*
>
> **World-class pentathlete Gwen Wentland**

DEVELOPING A RACE IMAGERY PROGRAM

A race imagery program allows racers to systematically address key areas they need to improve in their ski racing. Racers can use race imagery to consistently develop technical, tactical, and mental aspects of their skiing.

Race imagery goals. The first step in developing a race imagery program is to set goals. They could be technical, such as improving a technical part of your skiing, tactical, such as skiing a better line, mental, such as increasing your confidence or reducing your intensity, or relate to overall race performance, such as improving your consistency. Use the Race Imagery Goals form (see page 130) to identify the areas on which you want to work.

RACE IMAGERY GOALS

Name _____   **Date** _____

Directions: In the space below, indicate your goals for your race imagery program. Be specific in identifying areas where you want to improve your skiing.

Technical

    1.

    2.

Tactical

    1.

    2.

Mental

    1.

    2.

Overall Performance

    1.

    2.

Race imagery ladder. The next step involves creating a race imagery performance ladder. Racers wouldn't begin to change a part of their skiing in an important race. Rather, they would start by practicing new skills in a training situation where mistakes don't matter. Similarly, racers don't want to begin their race imagery program in a big imagined race. Using the Race Imagery Ladder form (see page 132), create a ladder of training and race situations in which you'll be skiing. The ladder should start with the least important training situation and increase up to the most important race in which you will ski. For example, a low rung of the Race Imagery Ladder could be training early in the season well before any important races and the highest rung could be competing in a championship race. This ladder enables you to work on areas you've identified in increasingly more demanding situations.

You should begin your race imagery program at the lowest rung of the ladder and work your way up until you've reached the highest rung. Don't move up to the next rung until you can ski the way you want at the current rung. Once you feel good at a particular rung, stay there for several imagery sessions to reinforce the positive images, thoughts, and feelings.

RACE IMAGERY LADDER

Name _____   **Date** _____

Directions: In the space below, create a ladder of training and race situations in which you will imagine yourself. The ladder should increase incrementally in terms of importance. Specify the skiing situation (e.g., free skiing, training, or race). Examples are italicized.

Least Important

     1. *(free skiing)*

     2. *(early season training)*

Moderately Important

     3. *(timed training runs)*

     4. *(low-level race)*

Most Important

     5. *(major race)*

Create race imagery scenarios. Once you've established your goals and built your race imagery ladder, you're ready to create training and race scenarios that you will follow in your race imagery sessions (see Race Imagery Scenarios on page 136). These scenarios are actual training or race situations in which you can work on your technical, tactical, mental, and performance goals.

The race imagery scenarios should mirror actual training and race experiences. For example, imagine yourself taking five GS training runs on your home hill or imagine yourself competing in a slalom on a race hill you have skied on before. These scenarios should provide you with detailed step-by-step descriptions of what you imagine doing from the start to the conclusion of the imagined training session or race.

You can use the Sample Training Scenario (see page 134) and Sample Race Scenario (see page 135) as guides in creating your own personalized race imagery scenarios. From these scenarios, add training and race elements that are unique to you such as your pre-race routine, particular warm-up exercises, and techniques to help you achieve prime focus and prime intensity.

It's important that your imagery scenarios are training or race specific. You shouldn't just imagine yourself skiing in a nonspecific location, event, and under undefined conditions. Rather, you should imagine a training or race scenario in which you ski at a particular site, in a specific event, against a identifiable field. Also, be sure that the events, locations, conditions, and level of competition are appropriate for your level of racing. For example, if you're a junior racer, you shouldn't imagine yourself competing against Kjetil Andre Aamodt or Kristina Koznick.

Practical concerns. You should structure your race imagery sessions into your daily routine. If you schedule them at the same time every day, you're more likely to remember to do them. Find a quiet, comfortable place where you won't be disturbed. Each session should last no longer than 10 minutes. Do race imagery three to four times a week. Like any form of training, if you do it too much, you'll get tired of it. Finally, start your race imagery sessions with one of the relaxation procedures that I described in Chapter Four. The deep state of relaxation will help you generate better quality images and it will make you more receptive to the images and feelings you're trying to ingrain.

SAMPLE TRAINING SCENARIO

You are in the start area before your first training run. You have a few racers to go before your run. It's time to get yourself totally prepared to ski your best.

Begin your pre-training routine. First, get your equipment ready. Buckle your boots, adjust your gear. Take a deep breath. [*pause 15 seconds*] Your equipment is prepared to ski your best.

It's now time to get yourself physically ready. Stretch out, warm-up your body, check and adjust your intensity. [*pause 15 seconds*] Take a deep breath. Your equipment is now totally ready for you to ski your best.

Two racers to go before your training run. It's time to get yourself mentally ready. Focus on what you want to work on this run. Close your eyes and imagine yourself skiing the way you want to. [*pause 15 seconds*] Take a deep breath. You are completely prepared to ski your best on this run.

In the gate, totally focused on skiing your best. Poles over the wand. Take a deep breath...GO. [*pause 30-90 seconds depending on the event*]

At the bottom of the training course. You had a great training run. You skied strong and fast. Now it's time to head back up for your next run.

On the ride up the lift, close your eyes and imagine yourself skiing the way you want on your next training run.

[*repeat scenario for each training run*]

SAMPLE RACE SCENARIO

Go out to the race hill. You're near the finish area about 30 minutes before your start. You've had a great week of training. You're skiing really well. You've inspected the course. You've taken your warm-up runs. You feel strong and fast. You will have a great race today.

It's time to go up for your run. Get on the lift and make your way to the top. On the ride up, close your eyes, take a deep breath, and see and feel yourself skiing strong and fast in your race run.

Off at the top of the lift, ski down to the start area, making fast, aggressive turns. [pause 15 seconds] Arriving at the start area, it's time to get yourself totally prepared to ski your best.

First, get your equipment ready, edges, bases, bindings. [pause 15 seconds] Take a deep breath. Your equipment is ready for you to ski your very best.

Now get yourself physically ready. Warm-up, stretch out, work up a sweat, make some turns. [pause 15 seconds] Take a deep breath. Your body is now totally prepared for you to ski your very best.

Five racers to go. Take off your outer wear, make your final adjustments, and buckle your boots. [pause 15 seconds] Take a deep breath.

Three racers to go. Get yourself mentally ready. Check and adjust your intensity. Imagine yourself skiing key parts of the course. [pause 15 seconds] Take a deep breath.

Time to go into race mode, totally focused on one thing: skiing as fast as you can. You will have a great race today

The starter calls you to the start. Slide your skis back and forth. Take a deep breath. Poles over the wand. Five seconds. Ready…GO. [Pause 45 seconds, SL; 65, GS; 75 SG; 90 DH]

In the finish area. You had a great run. Look back up the hill and review your run with race imagery. You skied really well, strong and fast. You are happy and excited. Remember that feeling. Remember what it feels like to ski your very best. When you race again, you can call upon those feelings and they will enable you to ski your best.

[repeat for two-run events]

RACE IMAGERY SCENARIOS

Name _____   **Date** _____

Directions: In the space below, create personalized training and race scenarios that you can follow in your race imagery sessions. These scenarios should provide you with detailed descriptions of what you want to imagine as you work on some part of your skiing in training and races.

Training

Race

Race imagery log. Since race imagery is not tangible like, for example, weight lifting where you can see how much weight you've lifted or sprints where you can be timed, it's useful to keep a log of your race imagery sessions. By recording your race imagery sessions, you'll be able to see improvement as you make your way up the ladder. Use the Race Imagery Log (see page 138) to record relevant aspects of your imagery sessions.

The first piece of information you should record is the *rung* of the race imagery ladder. Place a number between one and five to indicate where you are in your climb up the ladder. Rate the *quality* of the imagery session on a 1-10 scale. How clear were the images, how well did you ski, how did you feel about the imagery session?

Describe your *performance*, that is, what you worked on and what you actually imagined during the imagery session. Specify the *number of mistakes* you made in the imagery session. Then indicate what *type of mistakes* you made most frequently.

Rate the quality of your *senses* in your imagery session. Assign yourself a 1-10 score for how clear was the visual, auditory, and physical imagery you experienced. Lastly, evaluate the *mental* aspects of your imagery by briefly describing relevant thoughts and emotions you had during your imagery session. The emphasis of this area should be on how positive or negative were your thoughts and emotions.

> *"I've discovered that numerous performers use the skill of mental rehearsal. They mentally run through important events before they happen."*
>
> **Psychologist Charles Garfield**

RACE IMAGERY LOG

DATE	LADDER: # of rung	QUALITY: 1-10	PERFORMANCE: What you imagined	CONTROL: # & type of errors	SENSES: Visual - Auditory - Physical	MENTAL: Thoughts and emotions

CHAPTER TEN:

LESSONS LEARNED FROM THE WORLD CUP

Prime Time is what ski racing are all about. It's the reason why you work so hard on all aspects of your skiing. Prime Time is the reason you're reading this book. The goal of Prime Ski Racing is for you to ski your best in Prime Time. Prime Time refers to the most important races against the toughest field you will face.

Prime Time is that moment that defines you as a ski racer. It shows you and others how skilled you are, how well conditioned you are, and, most importantly, how strong you are mentally. This book has been directed toward you achieving Prime Ski Racing and being able to use it in Prime Time.

This notion of Prime Time emerged from my work with one young ski racer who was making a difficult, though successful, transition from high-level junior racing to the World Cup. What became clear to both of us was that the World Cup holds little resemblance to junior racing. The World Cup racers don't just do things better, they do things differently. These lessons that we learned together helped this racer overcome the challenges of world-class ski racing and progress up the world rankings. They also showed me things that racers at all levels could use to raise their level of skiing and achieve their highest level of ski racing success. These lessons are divided into categories: competitive and mental.

COMPETITIVE LESSONS

1.   *Ski to the best of your ability.* In any given race, you may not be at your best. You may not be skiing that well due to fatigue, illness, injury, or any number of reasons. Whatever ability you bring to the race, ski to the best of that ability. An important lesson I learned from working with world-class racers is that you can't always ski at 100%. Imagine the life of a World Cup racer. They travel and compete constantly, sometimes going from one side of the world to the other and having to compete the next day. There is simply no way they can be totally on top of their skis for every race.

Many times, before a race, racers just don't feel very good, and know they're not going to ski well. Because they're not going to ski at 100%, they, in essence, throw in the towel before the race even begins. They think, "If I'm not feeling good, there's no way I can ski well and get a good result. So why even try."

However, you don't have to ski your best to get a good result. You only need to ski better than your competition. So, to increase the likelihood of that happening, you must learn to ski your best with what you have on that given day. For example, if you're only at 80%, ski at the full 80%. That may still be enough for you to get a good result.

2.   *KISS.* Ski racing is really pretty simple. Whoever goes the fastest wins the race. Yet, racers can make ski racing complicated by trying to do too many things. A rule to follow is the KISS principle. Most racers know the KISS principle as "keep it simple stupid," but I don't believe that one. I believe racers should "keep it simple SMART!"

My KISS principle means that you should choose a few basic things you want to do in a race and stick to them. When things aren't going well, there can be a tendency to think too much and try to find some complex solution to the problem. This approach usually just clouds the situation and makes it worse.

Your goal should be to focus on a few things and do them to the best of your ability. In fact, on race day, the simplest of the KISS principle you should focus on is this: Go as fast as you can.

3. Expect it to be hard. This is one of the toughest lessons for young racers who are making the transition from the juniors to the world-class ranks. As juniors, there are always easy races. Because they are at such a high level, they will often be competing against racers who have much less ability. Not at the world-class level. Every race is hard. Every race is one they could lose because their competition is just as good, just as competitive, and just as hungry to win.

Races should be difficult. That is what makes it so much fun and rewarding. If you ski against a field that you are considerably better than and you win, how do you feel? Not much sense of accomplishment and satisfaction, is there? Races are supposed to be hard. They should be physically demanding. Races should test your technical and tactical capabilities. They should show you what you are made of mentally and emotionally. That is why you compete. This is even more true when you ski in Prime Time.

If you expect it to be hard, then there will be no surprises. If you fall behind after the first run, well, that is part of ski racing. If you choke, well, that happens. If you fight as hard as you can and still lose, well, you can still feel good for having given your best effort. If you expect it to be hard, you will prepare yourself physically and mentally for the demands of ski racing. When the race proves that you were right, it is tough, then you'll respond well and ski your best.

4. Win the mental race. As I alluded to in the preface, when you begin a race, you compete in two races. First, you compete against the field in the actual race. Second, you compete against yourself in the mental race. Your competition has a similar situation. Given fairly equal ability, whoever wins the mental race will win the actual race.

There are several keys to winning the mental race. Most importantly, you have to be your best ally rather than your worst enemy. If your competition is against you and you are against you, you don't have a chance. Another key is to never give up. Remember what happens when you give up; you automatically lose. As long as you stay motivated and keep fighting no matter how you're skiing, you will always have a chance. Two essential mental skills are to maintain prime focus and intensity throughout the competition. Without these two Prime Ski Racing skills, you will not be physically or mentally capable of skiing your best. This entire book is designed to help you win the mental race.

> *"It's all mental at this level, and most of the time, that's what hurts you. If you have a good attitude, you have a good chance."*
>
> **Casey Puckett**

MENTAL LESSONS

1.   *Believe in your ability.* As Chapter Three suggests, developing confidence in their ability is one of the biggest challenges racers face. Except for the very best in the world, many racers don't have that deeply ingrained belief in their capabilities. I see this often in races. For example, a racer makes a mistake early in a race run and then gives less than full effort the rest of the course because he has lost confidence in himself and he figures he has already lost the race.

This confidence in their ability is an essential quality that separates the great racers from the good ones. Through experience and success, they gain such trust in their capabilities that even when they are not skiing well, they keep going for it. They have such confidence that they know that if they just keep trying and not allow themselves to become tentative, they can still have a good race.

It's a mistake for the racer in the last example to give up just because he isn't skiing his best. Instead, this racer should keep fighting and try to ski his best the remainder of the course. The lesson you can take from the world's best racers is to believe in your ability and know that it will, in time, enable you to ski your best.

This belief will also serve you well in Prime Time. Imagine skiing your best. You have probably had many great training and race runs. Yet, the essential question is, Can you ski that well in the most important race of your life against the toughest field of competitors you have ever faced? The objective of Prime Ski Racing is to be able to ski your best when it really counts. This means being able to ski your best in Prime Time. The lesson you can learn from World Cup racers is to develop such a belief in your skiing that you truly know that you can ski your best when you absolutely need to. This belief in your skiing gives you the confidence to go for it in Prime Time.

2.   *Expect to be nervous in Prime Time.* Prime Time means the race in which you are competing matters. The race may be the Junior Olympics or the World Championships. You may start to feel nervous because it's an important race. This anxiety makes you uncomfortable, which raises doubts in your mind, causes you to feel negative emotions, and, because of all of these, you become more nervous. As a result, the quality of your skiing declines and you have a poor race.

This reaction is common among racers of all levels of ability. It is also one of the most harmful to Prime Ski Racing. Much of this book is directed toward helping you achieve prime intensity and not experience anxiety under pressure. The reality is, though, getting nervous before important races is normal and natural. It happens to club racers and it happens to the best racers in the world.

One way to partially alleviate the negative effects of this nervousness is to expect be to nervous in Prime Time. If you anticipate experiencing some anxiety, when it arises, your reaction will be, "This is normal. I knew I would get a little nervous. No big deal," instead of "Oh no. I can't believe I'm getting nervous now. How can I ski well feeling this way?"

Anxiety can also be interpreted in different ways producing very different reactions. If you view anxiety as negative and threatening, it will clearly hurt your skiing. If you see it, instead, as an indication that you're getting yourself prepared for the big race or the next race run, that the feeling is not anxiety, but rather getting psyched up, then you will see it much more positively. With a more positive perspective on the added intensity, it will be less likely to produce negative thoughts and emotions, and, as a result, it will have a less harmful effect on your skiing.

Another important realization is that whatever you're feeling, your competition is probably feeling the same doubts, anxiety, and emotions. Even if they look cool, calm, and collected on the outside, the chances are they're equally as nervous on the inside. This perspective offers even more support for the need to win the mental race. Given fairly equal ability, the racer who wins the mental race is most likely going to ski well and have a good result.

3. *Recover from mistakes quickly.* If you recall, Prime Ski Racing is based on the notion that you can ski at a consistently high level under challenging conditions. However, skiing consistently does not mean that you will not make mistakes or experience declines in your skiing. One of the things that makes World Cup racers so good is not that they don't make mistakes, but rather how quickly they recover from them. Races are often won or lost based on which racer can recover from their errors most quickly.

It's not uncommon for racers to take up to five gates or more to recover from a mistake on course such as sliding off line or hooking an arm on a gate. This occurs because racers lose confidence, focus, and intensity, and they become frustrated, angry, or depressed due to their mistakes. These negative emotions can, in turn, hurt their focus and intensity. This negative scenario may then produce a vicious cycle of poor skiing. It can take a while for them to get their head and their skiing together again and get back into the race. Unfortunately, by the time they recover mentally and raise their skiing to its previous level, the race may be lost.

Recovering from mistakes quickly begins with a forgiving attitude in which you accept that you will make mistakes and you understand that negative thoughts and emotions, and poor focus and intensity will cause you to ski worse. Accepting mistakes as part of ski racing will make it easier for you to let go of the mistakes

With the negative impact of mistakes reduced, you can then direct your attention to getting yourself back mentally and emotionally. This process begins with maintaining your confidence with positive thinking. You can then redirect your focus onto the process and the present, in other words, what you need to do now to improve your skiing and get back to attacking the course.

4.   *Accept the challenge.* The biggest obstacle to Prime Ski Racing is fear. Fear produces in racers a cautious attitude and tentative skiing. On a practical level, this means that their main goal is to just get down the hill in one piece. Racers don't ski the most aggressive line, become tentative on tough sections of the course, and hold back when speeds get too high.

There are few things more unsatisfying than going down with a whimper, not a bang. Racers usually feel terrible when they ski scared and they regret having skied so cautiously. Many racers often would rather fall while going for it than finish when skiing slowly.

Accepting the challenge means that you give it everything you have. You direct your fullest energy and effort into skiing as well as you can and going as fast as you are capable.

Before a race, accept the challenge to ski with courage and the willingness to risk in order to achieve Prime Ski Racing. Resolve to ski to your fullest ability. Commit to doing everything you can to ski your best. Accept that when you have this attitude, you won't always ski your best and have a good result. Understand that in Prime Time you can't always control whether you win or lose, but you can control the effort you put in, how hard you fight, and how well you ski. If you do that, then you're much more likely to achieve Prime Ski Racing and, win or lose, you will feel good about how you skied.

SECTION V:

PRIME SKI RACING PLAN

CHAPTER ELEVEN:

PRIME SKI RACING GOAL SETTING

Goal setting is essential to being the best ski racer you can be. Motivation is not enough to be your best. Motivation without goals is like knowing where you want to go without knowing how to get there. Goals act as the road map to your desired destination. Goals increase your commitment and motivation and provide deliberate steps toward your ski racing aspirations.

A Prime Ski Racing goal-setting program begins with a vision of where you want to go in your racing. It also provides a clear why, what, where, and how for your efforts in striving for Prime Ski Racing. The Prime Ski Racing Goal Formula (see below) illustrates the important role that goals play in becoming a better ski racer.

PRIME SKI RACING GOAL FORMULA

Motivation + Goals = P ROGRESS

TYPES OF GOALS

There are five types of goals that you want to set as part of your Prime Ski Racing goal-setting program. *Long-term* goals represent what you ultimately want to achieve in your ski racing such as to win the state championship, receive a skiing scholarship, or compete on the World Cup. *Yearly* goals indicate what you want to achieve in the next 12 months, for example, to attain a certain ranking or qualify for a particular race series. *Race* goals specify how you want to ski in specific races you'll be competing in during the coming year. *Training* goals represent what you need to do in your physical, technical, tactical, and mental training to achieve your race goals. *Lifestyle* goals indicate what you need to do in your general lifestyle to reach your goals such as sleep, diet, work or school, and relationships.

Lower goals should support and lead progressively to the higher goals. For example, your lifestyle goals should help you accomplish your training goals which, in turn, should lead to your race goals, which should enable you to reach your yearly goals which finally should allow you to achieve your long-term goals.

> *"Unless you're really dedicated to a goal, there's no point in doing it."*
>
> **Hilary Lindh**

GOAL GUIDELINES

The effectiveness of a Prime Ski Racing goal-setting program depends on whether you understand what kinds of goals to set and how to use them to enhance your motivation and direction. There are five goal guidelines you should follow to get the most out of your goal setting.

1. *Goals should be challenging, but realistic and attainable.* You should set goals that can be reached, but only with time and effort. If you set goals that are too easy, you'll reach them with little effort, so they do little for your motivation. If you set goals that are too difficult, you won't be able to achieve them no matter how hard you try. This wouldn't help your

motivation either since there would be little point in expending effort toward a goal you know you can't reach.

2. *Goals should be specific and concrete.* It's not sufficient to set a goal such as "I want to improve my leg strength." Goals should be clearly stated and measurable. For example, "I want to increase my leg strength by 10%." This goal indicates the precise area to be worked on and the specific amount of improvement aimed for.

3. *Focus on degree of, rather than absolute, goal attainment.* An inevitable part of goal setting is that you won't reach all of your goals because it's not possible to accurately judge what is realistic for all goals. If you're only concerned with whether you reach a goal, you may perceive yourself as a failure if you're unable to do so. This response will invariably reduce rather than bolster your motivation. You should be more concerned with how much of the goal you achieve (degree of attainment) rather than whether or not you fully reach the goal (absolute attainment). Though you won't attain all of your goals, you will almost always improve toward a goal. With this perspective, if you don't reach a goal, but still improve 50% over the previous level, you're more likely to view yourself as having been successful in achieving the goal.

4. *Goal setting is a dynamic and fluid process.* Goal setting is a process that never ends. When one goal is achieved, you should set another goal that is higher or in a different direction to continually motivate yourself to improve. You should review your goals regularly, compare them to actual progress, and adjust them as needed. Because you won't be able to set goals with perfect accuracy, you must be open to making changes as needed. For example, goals that you reach more easily than expected should be immediately reset to a higher level. Conversely, if you set goals that were too difficult to achieve, you should modify them to a more realistic level.

5. *Prepare a written contract.* Research suggests that goal setting is most effective when it's prepared as a written contract comprised of explicit statements of your goals and the specific way you will achieve them. This approach clearly identifies your goals and holds you

accountable for the fulfillment of the contract. You can complete a goal-setting contract, sign it, and give copies to your coach and others. To ensure that you continue to follow the contract, you can meet periodically with your coach to review your goals.

6.   *Get regular feedback.* One of the most important contributors to the effectiveness of a Prime Ski Racing goal-setting program is consistent feedback. You should get regular feedback about how you're doing in pursuing your goals. This information can come from coaches, video analysis, physical testing, or with Prime Ski Racing Profiling. Consistent feedback that you're reaching your goals and improving reinforces your motivation by showing you that your efforts are resulting in progress.

Using the Prime Ski Racing Goal Setting form (see page 153), write down your goals following the goal guidelines I just described. If you're uncertain of what your goals should be, ask your coach, your trainer, or others who know what you're working on.

"The resources of the human body and soul are enormous and beyond our present knowledge and expectations. We go part of the way to consciously tapping these resources by having goals that we want desperately."

Olympic track & field champion Herb Elliot

PRIME SKI RACING GOAL SETTING

Directions: In the space below, indicate your Long-term, Yearly, and Race goals.

Long-Team (ultimate ski racing dream):

Yearly (event qualification and ranking goals for the year):

Race (goals for specific races):

PRIME SKI RACING GOAL SETTING (cont.)

Directions: In the space below, set your Training and Lifestyle goals that will enable you to achieve your Race, Yearly, and Long-term goals. Also, under Method, indicate specifically how you will reach your Training and Lifestyle goals. Examples have been provided in *italics* for each type of goal.

Training (goals for all aspects of preparation):

Technical (*stance, body position, line)*

1.
   Method:

2.
   Method:

3.
   Method:

Physical (*strength, stamina, agility*)

1.
   Method:

2.
   Method:

3.
   Method:

PRIME SKI RACING GOAL SETTING (cont.)

Mental (*motivation, confidence, intensity, focus, emotions*)

    1.

       Method:

    2.

       Method:

    3.

       Method:

Lifestyle (sleep, diet, work/school, relationships):

    1.

       Method:

    2.

       Method:

    3.

       Method:

CHAPTER TWELVE:

PRIME SKI RACING PROGRAM

You now know what are your goals. The aim of the Prime Ski Racing program is to help you achieve these goals in the most efficient and organized way possible. You can develop your own individualized Prime Ski Racing program by following three steps: design, implementation, and maintenance.

DESIGN

The first thing you must do in the *design* phase of developing your Prime Ski Racing program is to identify your most crucial mental needs. You can use the results from your Prime Ski Racing profile to help you specify what mental areas you need to work on most. You'll also have different areas you need to work on in different ski racing settings. For example, focus might be most important when you're training, developing your race imagery skills may be most necessary off-hill, and controlling your intensity may be most critical on race day. Using the Prime Ski Racing Identification form (see page 158), list the mental areas that you want to focus on in training, off-hill, and on race day.

The next thing you need to do in designing your Prime Ski Racing program is to specify Prime Ski Racing techniques you will use to develop the mental areas you've just identified. It's not feasible to use every Prime Ski Racing technique for a certain area. For example, I described six strategies you could use to build your confidence. You should narrow those choices to two or three techniques that you like most. To do this, experiment with the different techniques for a few days and see which ones you're most comfortable with. Once again using the Prime Ski Racing Identification form, list the two or three techniques you've chosen. I recommend that race imagery be a regular part of your off-hill Prime Ski Racing program because it offers so many benefits to every mental area.

The final part of the design phase is to organize your Prime Ski Racing program into a daily and weekly schedule. Just as you plan your physical and technical training, you want to specify when you will be doing your Prime Ski Racing training. The Typical Prime Ski Racing Program (see page 159) illustrates how you can organize Prime Ski Racing techniques into a cohesive program. Using the Prime Ski Racing Planner (see page 161), indicate when and where you will use Prime Ski Racing techniques you've specified in the Prime Ski Racing Identification form.

> *"We need to know where we are going, and how we plan to get there. Our dreams and aspirations must be translated into real and tangible goals, with priorities and a time frame. All of these should be in writing, so that it can be reviewed, updated, and revised as necessary."*
>
> **former NFL great Merlin Olsen**

PRIME SKI RACING IDENTIFICATION

Directions: In the space below, indicate the mental areas on which you need to work in the different settings. Then, specify Prime Ski Racing techniques you will use to develop these areas.

Setting	Mental Area	Prime Ski Racing Techniques
Training		
1.		
2.		
3.		
Off-Hill		
1.		
2.		
3.		
Race Day		
1.		
2.		
3.		

TYPICAL PRIME SKI RACING PROGRAM

Mental Need and Goal	Mental Technique	Place in Schedule
Increase Motivation	Goal setting	Before season; monthly
	Two daily questions	At start and end of day
Build Confidence	Ski Racer's Litany	At start and end of training
	Thought-stopping	In training and and at races
Intensity Control	Deep breathing	During training and before races
	Active relaxation	At end of training
	Race routines	Training, pre-race
Overall Performance	Race imagery	Three times per week before dinner

IMPLEMENTATION

The second phase of the Prime Ski Racing program is *implementation*. This is where you put into action the Prime Ski Racing program you've just designed. It's best that you begin your Prime Ski Racing program as far in advance of race season as possible. There are several benefits to starting your Prime Ski Racing program early. It enables you to develop the most effective Prime Ski Racing program possible. An early start allows you to incorporate it fully into your overall training program. It lets you fine-tune the program to best suit your needs. Most importantly, it gives you the time to practice the skills and gain its benefits.

A concern that racers often have is the time commitment required for a Prime Ski Racing program. Certainly, they are busy enough without introducing one more thing into their lives, no matter how important it is. Racers can spend hours every day in their physical and technical training and there simply wouldn't be similar time to devote to their Prime Ski Racing program. Fortunately, Prime Ski Racing training doesn't require hours a day to gain its benefits. Most Prime Ski Racing training can be incorporated directly into a traditional on- and off-hill training program. Only about 10-15 minutes a day extra is needed for outside Prime Ski Racing training such as relaxation and race imagery.

If you feel that all of the areas and techniques you've identified in your Prime Ski Racing program are too much to do, then start small. Select half the techniques you've specified and work on those. You'll find that Prime Ski Racing training is not only not time consuming or overwhelming, but rather it is an enjoyable addition to your current training program and a nice break from your usual routine. You'll also find that you pick up Prime Ski Racing techniques quickly and you'll get to the point where you do them with little thought.

PRIME SKI RACING PLANNER

Time	Monday	Tuesday	Wednesday	Thursday	Friday	Saturday	Sunday
MORNING							
AFTERNOON							
EVENING							

MAINTENANCE

The final phase of the Prime Ski Racing program is *maintenance*. The reality is that there is no end to the use of Prime Ski Racing training. Just like physical conditioning and technical skills, mental skills will atrophy when they're not maintained through regular use. As I described in the Positive Change Formula, repetition is essential for you to maintain Prime Ski Racing. Fortunately, with training, Prime Ski Racing skills become automatic, so you need less time and effort to retain them. For example, once you've developed your focus skills, it's easier to stay focused, so you don't have to pay as much attention to your focusing techniques.

Once you achieve Prime Ski Racing, you can adjust your Prime Ski Racing program to a lower, though still consistent, level of involvement. Also, as new problems arise, you can modify your Prime Ski Racing program to resolve them.

POSTSCRIPT

To be motivated, confident, intense, and focused. To be an emotional master. To be your best ally in your ski racing rather than your worst enemy. To ski your best consistently under the most challenging conditions. These are the skills that Prime Ski Racing can help you develop.

Why is Prime Ski Racing so important to you that you would read this book and put such time and effort into your ski racing? Your answer is a personal one. For some, it may be to have more fun racing. For others, it may be to become the best ski racer they possibly can. For still others, it may be to win more races.

I would like to believe, though, that the most compelling reason why you want to achieve Prime Ski Racing is to master what I have described as the most important and difficult race in which you compete, in your ski racing and in your life. That race is the *mental race*. If you can win the mental race and remove all of the obstacles that keep you from skiing your best and living your fullest life, then everything is possible.

By winning the mental race, you clear the path to happiness, fulfillment, and success in ski racing and, yes, in life. I hope that, as you have read *Prime Ski Racing*, you've thought, "Hey, this could apply to my work" or "This relates to my relationships." Ski racing, like life, is filled with challenges, struggles, excitement, setbacks, failures, and ultimately, mastery. Because to experience the "triumph of the racer's mind" is also to seize victory in the race of life.

Jim Taylor, Ph.D.
September, 2000

References

Apter, M. J. (1989). *Reversal theory: Motivation, emotion, and personality.* London: Routledge.

Butler, R. J., & Hardy, L. (1992). The performance profile: Theory and application. *The Sport Psychologist, 6,* 253-264.

Cautela, J. R., & Wisocki, P. A. (1977). Thought-stoppage procedure: Description, application, and learning theory applications. *Psychological Records, 27,* 255-264.

Ericsson, K., & Charnes, N. (1994). Expert performance: Its structure and acquisition. *American Psychologist, 49,* 725-747.

Jacobson, E. (1930). *Progressive relaxation.* Chicago: University of Chicago.

Moran, A. (1996). *The psychology of concentration in sport performers*: A cognitive analysis. East Sussex, UK: Psychology.

Nideffer, R. M. (1981). *The ethics and training of applied sport psychology.* Ithaca, NY: Mouvement.

Singer, R. N., Murphey, M., & Tennant, L. K. (Eds.). (1993). *Handbook of research on sport psychology.* New York: MacMillan.

Taylor, J. (1996). *The mental edge for sports* (4th ed.). Denver, CO: Minuteman.

Van Raalte, J. L., & Brewer, B. W. (Eds.). (1996). *Exploring sport and exercise psychology*. Washington, DC: APA.

Williams, J. M. (Ed.). (1998). *Applied sport psychology: Personal growth to peak races* (3rd ed.) (pp. 219-236). Palo Alto, CA Mayfield.

About the Author

Jim Taylor, Ph.D., is a sport psychologist widely recognized for his work in the psychology of ski racing. He has been a consultant to the U.S. and Japanese Ski Teams, the U.S. Ski Coaches Association, and has worked with World Cup, Olympic, and professional racers, and many of the top junior race programs in the U.S. Dr. Taylor received his bachelor's degree from Middlebury College and earned his M.A. and Ph.D. in Psychology from the University of Colorado. He is a former associate professor and Director of Sport Psychology at Nova University in Ft. Lauderdale. A graduate of Burke Mountain Academy, Dr. Taylor held a top-20 national slalom ranking, competed internationally, captained the 1981 NCAA 5th-ranked Middlebury College Ski Team, was a member of the 1982 NCAA Champion University of Colorado Ski Team, and competed on the professional ski tour. He is a 2nd degree black belt in karate and a marathon runner. Dr. Taylor is the author of thirteen books including the *Prime Sport* book series and *Psychological Approaches to Sports Injury Rehabilitation*, has published over 220 articles in popular and professional publications, and has been a regular contributor to *Ski Racing* and *American Ski Coach*. He has given more than 300 workshops to athletes, coaches, and parents in the U.S., Canada, and in Europe.

Printed in the United States
29687LVS00003B/217-219